Plundertown, U.S.A.

For Dave

*Thanks so much
for your interest.*

*Al Sanders
Dec 2003*

"Them leave sorrow, tears and blood/Them regular trademarks."

Felá Anikulapo-Kuti*

* "Sorrow, Tears and Blood" (Felá Anikulapo), ©EMI Virgin Music Pub. France/EMI Music Pub. Yaba/FKO Music

Plundertown, U.S.A.

Coos Bay Enters the Global Economy

Al Sandine

ISBN 0-88839-525-6

Cataloging in Publication Data

Sandine, Al, 1938-
  Plundertown, USA

  Includes bibliographical references and index.
  ISBN 0-88839-525-6

1. Coos Bay Region (Or.)—History. 2. Coos Bay Region (Or.)—
Economic conditions. I. Title.
F882.C7S26 2003   979.5'23   C2003-910447-8

Printed in Indonesia—TK PRINTING

Editor: Lesley Cameron
Production: Bob Canlas
Cover design: Theodora Kobald
Front cover photo: Gordon Ross
Back cover photo: Shirley Richards

*We acknowledge the financial support of the Government of Canada through the
Book Publishing Industry Development Program (BPIDP) for our publishing activities.*

Published simultaneously in Canada and the United States by

HANCOCK HOUSE PUBLISHERS LTD.
19313 Zero Avenue, Surrey, B.C. V3S 9R9
(604) 538-1114 Fax (604) 538-2262

HANCOCK HOUSE PUBLISHERS
1431 Harrison Avenue, Blaine, WA 98230-5005
(604) 538-1114 Fax (604) 538-2262
Web Site: www.hancockhouse.com *email:* sales@hancockhouse.com

Contents

Illustrations

Acknowledgments and Dedication

I could not have written this book without the help of several other people. First was my sister-in-law, Jane B. Wilson, who gave me a telephone introduction to Ardella Edwards. Ardella provided me with lots of factual material regarding local employment as well as a telling quote. My friend of more decades than either of us can easily recall, Bob Beggs, gave me valuable support without even knowing it, just by getting excited by some of the Coos Bay stories that I shared with him over dinner one night. Three generations of peer counselors at the Berkeley Free Clinic have had to listen to my check-ins about "the book." All have been entirely sympathetic, I believe. Also, during Plundertown's long gestation period, Isaiah Smithson was enormously generous with his time, interest, knowledge, and critical acumen. Printouts of our long emails from 1999 continue to turn up.

At the later end of the process, Aya Suzuki of the University of California's geography department produced a terrific map. David Glick has provided his continuing example of political commitment and a friendship that warms my life. I also thank Larry Shoup for the ideas he contributed to the Epilogue and his openness to my ideas.

Mary Bradford has long suffered my frustrations and shared my joys. I've been able to consolidate and focus such feelings on the writing and marketing of this book in recent years, making it emotionally economical for me but not any easier for her. Besides her constant support, she provided a final edit and style critique.

Capping all other help was that of my friend, Ariel Dorfman. Without his influence and advice, communicated in the course of cross-country phone calls and walks under Duke's near-leafless trees a couple of falls ago, I would by now have buried myself beneath a mountain of three-by-five note cards and reading lists. His encouragement has supported my every step from inspiration to publication.

IN CHAPTER 13 I mention a last visit to Coos Bay. It was the last visit at the time. Needing to collect photographs, I returned in March 2002. The people I met with at that time, those who had responded to my advertisement for photographs of the area—Dick Kimker, Rich Kuznitsky, Shirley Richards, Gordon Ross, and Mike Vaughan—turned out to be so giving of their time and (in the case of four of them) so generous with their photographs that I was touched. Through them I felt a connection with Coos Bay that no amount of research and memory could ever provide.

Of course, if you own photographs of historical interest you ought to consider giving them to your local historical society—in the case of Coos Bay, this is the Coos Historical Museum. Better the museum than letting your treasures get eaten by little critters in the back of a descendant's drawer.

FINALLY, I DEDICATE THIS BOOK to my brothers and sister, who participated in some of its contents, and to my brothers and sisters at Coos Bay, who have had to actually bear the impact of events that I only write about.

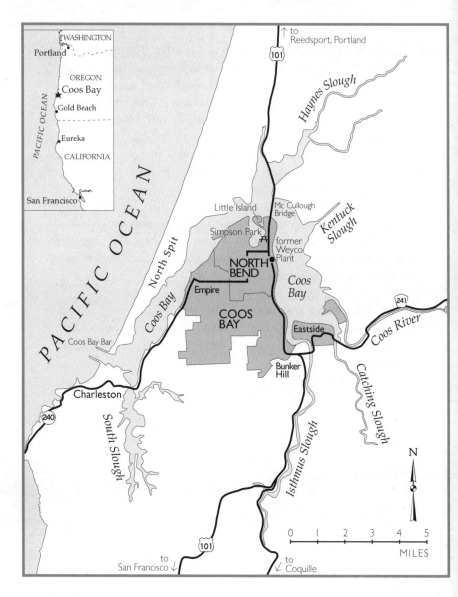

Coos Bay area

CHAPTER 1

Stumped

IT WAS IN THE FALL OF **1998**, and I was in the fall of life, driving south through Oregon on Interstate 5, heading for my home in California after a trip to Seattle to visit my son. Past Eugene I took the turn-off for the Umpqua River route to the coast. I was looking forward to the chance to see the Coos Bay area again—I would spend the night in North Bend, where I'd lived until my family left the area in 1952 when I was fourteen.

The river route is pleasant after Drain, where I had stopped to fuel up: gas for the car, caffeine for me. Drain had a semi-pro baseball team that used to play our Lumberjacks. The Black Sox they were called, and they were pretty good. More memories came crowding in as I shot by Ten Mile Lake on Highway 101. My father used to take us fishing here on weekends, and it was here at Lakeside that I learned to swim. How I used to dread that fourteen-mile drive from North Bend. Going to my doom, I thought. Because of the curvy road, I always got car-sick. My father used to sneer that it was all in my head.

A lot of things *are* in my head these days: information and ideas regarding something big and sad that happened to this area I lived in as a kid. And like the nausea of car-sickness, I can't keep it to myself.

I situate my favorite childhood memories on a mental map, a map of trails in the woods across the unpaved street from where we used to live. One trail in particular comes to mind. It went along a wooded ridge where we could hear the tidal mutterings below and catch whiffs of skunk cabbage. Somebody would always have something to say about the smell, of course. I can just about imagine our reaction if somebody had told us that people used to make a meal out of young skunk cabbage roots. I didn't know that, not as a boy of six nor as a man of sixty driving toward Coos Bay in 1998. But I know now that lots of people did just that. They may even have harvested roots from that very same patch.

At the end of the skunk cabbage trail was a certain stump. Rifle cartridges studded its top. Big ones, little ones: a sharp ten-year-old could name the calibers. But that got old. Soon we would scoot down the path to the railroad tracks. From here we would usually head right, walking toward familiar possibilities, such as the clay mine under the bridge above the tracks. To the left lay a more ambitious possibility, but we won't go there for now.

Once in a while, instead of following the tracks, we crossed them to the woods on the other side. These woods weren't like our woods. They were dark and forbidding. At their heart, thick growth enclosed a scummy greenish pond. Once as we were running out of there my brother fell and cut his palm on a half-buried shard of blue glass. He had to have his hand stitched.

I hardly remember anything about my classroom experience, but I remember sauntering through the quiet streets of North Bend's only suburb, Simpson Heights. Passing the last of the big houses, we would come to a road, unused and overgrown with blackberry vines. I remember the first time someone talked me into tasting one of the green stalks that also grew in great profusion there. Ah, licorice, said my mouth. I wondered how it could come from such an unlicorice-looking source.

The short road took us to a spot on the bay where other people didn't come, for other people had no business there. Or maybe I should say, other people had business, whereas we had adventures and fun. As I recall the rotting pilings and the smell, which I now recognize as creosote, I realize that this was probably the spot where Asa Simpson had his lumber mill, his shipyard, and his white-capped company town. (We'll run into him in Chapter 3.) Around 1948, when we favored the site, there were only scraps remaining of the operation that had started North Bend up.

For us it was a place to savor anise stalks, chuck stones into the choppy bay, and scrutinize any passing ship. On the other side was Kentuck Slough, where my father had grown up on a farm, working almost round the clock, from what he said. Our cousins still had a dairy farm over there. Tumbling in their hayloft was a major experience in the realm of fun. From where we sat in Simpson Heights, Kentuck was just a bluish line of trees. Not old-growth, of course. The trees along the bay had been the first to go.

SUCH WAS THE FLAVOR of my memories as I approached Coos Bay. But straight and fast the present highway runs. I got to old McCullough Bridge so soon I hadn't time to calculate or even ask myself how many times I might have crossed that bridge by car and bike and foot. Then I was checking into a motel just a couple of short blocks from where we used to live. In fact, my boyhood friends and I had seen it built. "*Motel?*" we'd asked. "What's that?"

Soon I took the obligatory walk to stretch my legs and stand for a moment before the house with the gambrel roof, looking spiffy after all these years. It was the house in which my father, too, had lived as a boy and purchased and refurbished as a man. No point in lingering: nothing that could happen now would hold a candle to what had happened some years back when I was in the area with Mary, my partner. While the two of us were standing there, a woman had come out of the house. As she was smiling, I explained that I'd lived in that very house as a boy. She knew of my family and was kind enough to ask us in. So in we went, and immediately I was thrilled to see my father's fine handicraft in knotty cabinets and moldings. We went upstairs, and in an all but forgotten room that once was mine I saw, in the closet, a strip of old forgotten wallpaper. It was gray and patterned with battleships. World War II, you know. As I went downstairs again, my chest was full of the realization that I didn't just dream it up. My childhood had really happened—and right here!

As nothing like that was likely to occur again, I decided to take a walk through town. Although I'd been in the area once or twice since 1952, I'd been preoccupied with other things, and so I didn't really have a sense of what had changed. I wasn't expecting to find the North Bend of five decades back, of course but still, I was shocked. The façade of buildings lining Sherman Avenue, North Bend's main drag, had gaps like missing teeth. A person no longer had to go to the end of the block to see the bay. Of the remaining businesses, what I saw were mainly stores that sold used goods: used books, antiques, surplus goods, and bric-a-brac. I counted ten. There were empty storefronts too. "Sign-up for indoor paintball," said a fading sign in one. They had tried almost everything, it seemed.

It was such a contrast to the bustling downtown of my childhood. I could remember an insurance company office, a soda fountain, and a shoe store with an x-ray machine that turned your feet, inside the shoes that you were trying on, a ghastly glowing green. I remembered a Chinese grocer and a barbershop where I had had a painfully embarrassing experience which became a minor item in a local newspaper and which my mother clipped and put away like a tiny time bomb for me in a bottom drawer. And I certainly remembered the bus depot where, for five cents, you could take a bus to rival Coos Bay (born Marshfield), three miles to the south, and the Liberty Theater, where they had free movies every Saturday afternoon, plus a stage show. Every kid in town would make that scene.

The theater building was still there. Occasionally it held little theater programs, it appeared. But no more free movies on Saturday afternoon, that was for sure. All those other enterprises and many more besides had disappeared without a trace. Well, what could I expect after half a century? A few people on the street might be nice. Besides the ones in passing vehicles, the only members of the public I could find were livening up a bar. I went in there to find an ATM.

Was everybody shopping at the mall that occupies the wetland fill where we had sometimes gone to swim in water that was even colder than the lake's? No, I later found out that Pony Village, as it's called, was also lifeless and rundown. North Bend was just a shell of its former self. A shell? No, a shell doesn't feel pain. A sign I'd noted off the main street spoke of pain. Women's Crisis Services, it said.

Did I mention that I missed the noise? I hadn't known it at the time, but when we lived there the Coos Bay area was well on its way to being the "World's Largest Lumber Shipping Center." At least a billboard put up by the Port of Coos Bay in 1960 made that claim, and West Coast shipping data show that this was not just hype.[1] North Bend's screaming saws and piercing signals for the change of shift set up a background din to everything we did including sleep. But all was quiet now. The sounds of industry had been switched off. What I saw along the bay, where all the mills and factories had once stood, were stacks and stacks of smallish logs.

Thinking to learn more about North Bend's decline, I poked around and found that, in some respects, things were even worse than they appeared. The logs I'd seen along the bay would not even be rough-milled locally. They were caught in a bottleneck awaiting shipment to Japan. Coos Bay (the town) looked more or less okay, at least compared to North Bend. But information I collected from the Oregon Employment Department showed that the entire area had sustained a grievous wound, and the prognosis for early recovery was grim.

14

Change hadn't come overnight. Already by 1976, "things were starting to run out,"[2] but the nightmare from which Coos Bay residents have yet to awaken began in earnest around 1980, when an epidemic of wood products plant closures boosted the official jobless level up to nearly 15 percent. Locals of the millworkers' union, the International Woodworkers of America, went from a one-time high of 1,800 members down to around 200 by 1981. One local builder went six months without a call. He survived by getting the bank to let him maintain foreclosed properties in lieu of house payments.[3]

Dipped in a corrosive mix of alcohol and desperation, the social fabric fell apart. Homicide, rape, robbery, aggravated assault, burglary, larceny, car theft—reported incidents in all categories of crime shot up. It was as if Coos Bay had been hit by a plague affecting its prime wage earners first, then everybody else. Thousands left the area, but most stayed where they were.

I'm no sociologist, but it looked to me as if those who lost their jobs were male heads of household, typically, who lacked the skills, education, and social flexibility to avail themselves of new vocational opportunities in unfamiliar locales. These were not your city dudes. Lacking a legitimate outlet for his sense of outrage and despair, the one-time breadwinner might lash out blindly at the people nearest him. Wounded women and children swamped local services.[4]

The area has not come back, either economically or socially. The state's Economic & Community Development Department regards Coos County as a "distressed area."[5] Lumber exports stand at less than 5 percent of those of even ten years back. More than 4000 jobs in wood products industries have been lost. Piles of wood chips, the ingredients of future newspapers, rise along the bay in place of manufacturing plants that once ran triple shifts. Guarding vacancy against collective memory, chain-link fences indicate the sites of other missing mills.

Rampant problems of drug and alcohol abuse and domestic violence continue. Younger people with the chance to move out do so. Moving in are older folks, many of them needing medical services. In fact, my elderly mother-in-law died in a convalescent home in North Bend, having moved to the area to be near her daughter (my sister-in-law), who was brought to Coos Bay by a job with the state. A hospital has become the largest employer in the area; the only job growth is in low-paying service positions, mainly occupied by women. Like their cohorts everywhere else in the United States. these days, Coos Bay's female fast-food, cleaning, and elder- or child-care workers do the work that women of my mother's generation did at home. But they do it for low wages, and the beneficiaries of their efforts aren't other family members but strangers.[6]

Some call such employment the "affective face" of the process that has come to characterize so much of the formerly industrialized world.[7] The other face of jobs in the new economy consists of information services. In Chapter 12 we'll see how some former Coos Bay mill workers now occupy a lowly rung of the information-generating ranks.

When I asked people about the reasons for all this change, one person told me that it was because the big corporations had "strip-mined the forest" and then closed their plants. Others made vague references to market decline and "globalization," but all agreed that Coos Bay's forests had been depleted of commercially viable timber. Certain companies had treated Coos Bay as seventeenth-century pirates might have done a merchant ship.

But depletion? To deplete something means, at root, to empty it. I thought of the hollow stump in the woods across from where we used to live. It was big enough for five or six boys to climb inside of it. As a tree it must have been the biggest in the area. The only thing approaching it was an old yellow log at a nearby trail junction, a place we often stopped to ponder surface carvings of some earlier gang of boys. But that hollow stump has been gone for a long time now, its section of the woods torn out to make room for a tennis court.

Before I left North Bend I took another walk, north this time, away from the deadened downtown. The sight of Simpson Park heartened me. If only they'd left it alone. But at least it was still there. So was the bridge above the clay mine and the railroad tracks. From my vantage point parallel lines of tracks sped to a meeting at infinity. The rainwater pools next to them reflected salmon sky, and the roadbed had a ragged hem of green, green evergreens. Looking west along those tracks I also journeyed back in time, for had my body gone the same way as my eyes, I should have come at last to the Little Island.

The Little Island! It was nothing more than a windswept scrap of scrubby dunes, driftwood, and debris, but we were guaranteed to have it to ourselves. Now, a journey to the Little Island was not something we did casually. It meant packing sandwiches and water, first of all, for there would be no other food or drink once we got there. When we were underway at last and following the tracks, it meant disregarding all the warning signs that would have scared most other boys away. The danger was, once on the railroad bridge the only place to walk was on the ties. With just a few inches of margin on either side, there wasn't room for both a moving train and us. There were, of course, the u-shaped safety pockets in the guardrail that we came to every hundred feet or so. The question was, what would happen if a train came when we were between those pockets? Could we run fast enough to get to safety? Probably, but we never found that out, because one never did. Trains through there were few and far between.

What we did on the Island wasn't as important as the return journey. Here we had a choice. We might climb the ladder up to the tracks and walk back the way we'd come. Or, for a supreme adventure, we might go only halfway up, returning via the treacherous catwalk. One misstep on one of its connecting planks could put you waist-deep in the tidal muck fifteen feet below. It had happened to our neighbor Ralph. Things like that were always happening to Ralph. But I think now that we probably *talked* of taking the catwalk a lot more than we actually *took* the catwalk. That's the thing about adventures. They make for good talk.

Ah, the Little Island. But I soon resumed my walk. I was glad to see the forested lanes branching off from Sherman Avenue, where we used to ride our bikes. Some shaggy trees in there were ancient when my granddad was a pup. I descended the stairs that lead to McCullough Bridge's underside. I could remember my first time down there. Chalked on walls were the strangest drawings, obviously crude and aggressive, but what were they about? There was a moment in time when I didn't have a clue. Now it appeared that those crude samples of pornography had been painted over many times. It made me feel old, of course. I mean, not once or twice but many times!

But I'd forgotten the bridge's massive arches and the infinite regression that they give to somebody who stands in just the right spot. The child I used to be had probably never noticed that any more than, standing there that fall evening in 1998, I could know that soon I would be poring over faded photos of McCullough's half-built underparts, exposed for all the world to see when it was being built. The origins of McCullough Bridge would cease to be an unexamined mystery, and I would even learn the place of Ten Mile Lake in the economy of the indigenous inhabitants of Coos Bay. All this and much, much more.

As I DROVE AWAY FROM THE AREA, I thought of how Coos Bay and I had gone our separate ways. My father had moved us 200 miles south to Eureka, California, when I was fourteen. Within a couple of years I was discovering the joys and pain of alcohol and girls, flirting with trouble, and developing a lifelong taste for jazz. I seldom thought about Coos Bay and, on the rare occasions when I did, the area occupied a frozen past. While Coos Bay was busily becoming a world-class lumber port and acquiring a community college, I was becoming a scholar, starting a family before I was ready, and acquiring a rebellious attitude. My education didn't stop when I dropped out of a doctoral program. As Coos Bay's lumber mills and plywood plants were closing down, I was learning about uneven economic development throughout the world and the momentous shift from manufacturing to service jobs within the United States. I could spot a "supply region" a thousand miles away, at least on a map. By then Coos Bay's supply of things to sell the world was gone. Its economy had been mugged.

Coos Bay's geographic isolation was matched by my alienation from the existing social order. I was somehow immune from the general "state of anaesthesia from which all detrimental ideas tend to be excluded."[8] I dined on "detrimental ideas." To keep from choking, I became politically active. Meanwhile, I usually made a living toiling in the gut of California's workers' compensation system. On the wall of my cubicle was a photograph of another such toiler. Was that my son, someone asked once. In fact, Franz Kafka was not my son but my patron saint. As I discovered time and again to mounting frustration, the system had little to do with helping injured workers.

Now I'd found that in the heartland of my childhood memories almost every worker had been hurt, not by accidents but by deliberate decisions made somewhere else. Maybe I could do no more for them than I had for those caught up in the meshes of the California workers' compensation scheme, but I could do *something*. I could bear witness to what had happened at Coos Bay.

So, I began to read about the area, learning soon that in the 1980s economic disaster had visited the entire Pacific Northwest. Actually, "visited" is probably the wrong word. Economic disaster had come and set its scrawny self down hard on the region. One member

18

of Congress declared that the situation "rival[ed] the Great Depression." Another called it "the greatest environmental and economic crisis ever to confront the Pacific Northwest."[9] Because of its dependence on timber to the exclusion of almost everything else, no place had been sat on harder than Coos Bay. Oregon's leading newspaper called it "a cautionary example" for the entire region.[10]

Emerging from my preliminary research was a picture of a rusting mill site rendered from a palette full of blacks and grays and whitish blue, with only the occasional touch of burnt sienna for a bit of warmth. Resource depletion, plant closures, job flight: the picture suggested widespread areas of the country and indeed the world, for the changes I saw at Coos Bay were part of a general economic "restructuring" that was robbing workers all across the United States of the security of their jobs. Between 1980 and 1985, when the bulk of Coos Bay's plants shut down, 2.3 million manufacturing jobs were lost. (This according to the U. S. Department of Labor.[11]) A leading explanation went like this. Declining profits in the 1970s plus greatly reduced transportation and communications costs meant that "[i]ndustry that had traditionally been tied by locational constraints to raw material sources or markets could become much more footloose."[12] And it did. Thus, Coos Bay stood for Flint, Michigan; Youngstown and Akron, Ohio; Hopedale, Massachusetts; Anaconda, Montana; Johnstown, Pennsylvania; and many, many other once-bustling sites. What could be more important than what had happened at Coos Bay?

TWO MONTHS AFTER MY EPIPHANY under McCullough Bridge, I returned, driving north from the San Francisco Bay area into a driving rain, with a nasty head cold coming on. I stopped at the same motel again, taking a cramped but cheap room. Business was lousy, and there were three empty rooms on either side of mine: just what I needed for a good night's sleep.

When I went out for dinner, I found what appeared to be the only place on Sherman Avenue still serving a full meal, a Chinese restaurant. The crowd of standees just inside the door was much too clamorous, much too happy just to be in out of the cold, for me to want to stay. I went around the corner where the post office used to be and was surprised to find a Mexican cafe. It was quiet, the waitress was nice, and the food was plentiful if just about too hot. As I came out I noticed the gun shops next to it.

In the next few days I went to libraries, arranged a few interviews, tried to make contact with some relatives, took notes in my room, nibbled at Fernand Braudel's tome on the sixteenth-century Mediterranean world,[13] and nursed my terrible cold. Then, taking advantage of insomnia, I left Coos Bay early one morning in the dark. I faced a long drive home, but I felt charged by the freedom of being able to drive away from the place, a few questions answered but none asked of me. A little giddy when I stopped for gas at Coos Bay's south end, I chatted uncharacteristically with the gas pumper. Oh, yes, in Oregon they won't let you pump your own gas. An attendant has to do it for you, just like in the olden days when "service stations" provided some minimum of free customer service. Me, I love it.

A COUPLE OF THINGS about this book. One, I proceed on the assumption that in order to understand something that happened historically, you have to know what went before. In other words, I misspoke when I said, above, that the bad times began in the 1970s. The bad times are associated with *events* that began in the 1970s, but their roots go back much further than that, as we shall see. In this book, I try to do for events what the media so often fail to do: provide historical context.

Number two is a caveat. This book includes political opinions. It was motivated both by political passions and the occasional desire, shared by some, to return to childhood—the best of childhood, that is. But it was mainly inspired not by nostalgia but a sense of outrage. Not that I write angrily. The facts that I present speak for themselves. Although they often urge me to say more, I usually resist.

Number three is that the "we" of my childhood memories are my brothers and I and, at times, our neighborhood pals. When I say "Coos Bay," I mean the area, not the town, unless I signal otherwise. And if I sometimes refer to the "bay" and sometimes to the "estuary," please don't be confused. Coos Bay is really an estuary.

Finally, about the title of the book: I was going to call it "Catching Up With Coos Bay." But that's about me and my own personal experience. My friend Ariel advised "Plundertown, USA." "Plundertown" refers to Coos Bay's corporate plunderers. As for the people who've remained behind in their plundered towns, no mere book title can do them justice. They have to seek justice by other means. I'll get into that a bit in the final chapter.

ENDNOTES

1. Cf. *New York Times* August 21, 2000: A1, describing Coos Bay as formerly "the largest wood-products shipping port in the world."

2. Richard Kuznitski, personal interview, March 19, 2002.

3. Kuznitski interview.

4. See Foster Church, "G-P shutdown affects financial, mental health of community," Portland *Oregonian* January 26,1981; The [Coos Bay] *World* 9 February 1989: 1, 3.

5. <http://www.econ.state.or.us/DistList.htm>

6. Cf. Christine Kelly, "Muckraking in the Low-Wage World," rev. of *Nickel and Dimed: On (Not) Getting By in America* by Barbara Ehrenreich, *New Politics* 32.viii.4 (Winter 2002): 208-15.

7. Michael Hardt and Antonio Negri, *Empire* (Cambridge, Mass.: Harvard University Press, 2000) 293.

8. Herbert Marcuse, *Eros and Civilization: A Philosophical Inquiry into Freud* (Boston: Beacon Press, 1966) 104.

9. Jolene Unsoeld, D-WA, and Peter DeFazio, D-OR, quoted in *The World*, May 3,1991: 3.

10. Quoted in William Robbins, *Hard Times in Paradise: Coos Bay, Oregon, 1850-1986* (Seattle: University of Washington Press, 1988) 10.

11. Cited in Christian Parenti, "The 'New' Criminal Justice System: State Repression from 1968 to 2001," *Monthly Review* 53.3 (July–August 2001): 23.
12.*David Harvey, The Condition of Postmodernity: An Enquiry into the Origins of Cultural Change* (Cambridge, Mass.: Blackwell Publishers, 1990) 165.

13. The influence of Fernand Braudel shows up in Chapter 4.

CHAPTER 2

Borrowed Time

IT WAS 1944 when my father relocated us from balmy southern California to his rainy hometown on the Oregon coast. I remember frost on the planks when we walked to school in the morning, but walking on planks instead of asphalt was novelty enough! At first we stayed with my grandfather, whose English was a Swedish import that I couldn't understand. I got the chickenpox. No sooner was I over it than I tangled with a neighbor kid named Freddie Gum. It wasn't much of a fight. Extricating myself from his arms and legs, I hightailed it into my grandfather's house, pride battered by the jeers of witnesses.

My father made the house with the gambrel roof across from Simpson Park like new for us, and we moved in at last. Though still newcomers compared to our neighbors and the mud puddles that permanently pocked the unpaved street out front, it seemed by the following year that we had lived there all our lives. Then, merrily strolling down the hill from Central School one fine August afternoon, we heard the sound of church bells and the noontime siren's blast. Bells and siren in the middle of a weekday afternoon? Soon came people who were happy to explain. The war was over. It was the end of World War II. Having known nothing else, we thought that it was never going to end.

There was plenty for people at Coos Bay to celebrate. For those who suffered no personal loss, there was the war itself, which had brought Coos Bay, with the rest of the country, out of the economic doldrums and into a period of full employment. Government orders for lumber had taken off with Lend Lease; with Pearl Harbor they shot out of sight. Having often produced more wood than they could profitably sell, Coos Bay's mills suddenly couldn't produce enough.

And southwestern Oregon had one of the largest, if not *the* largest, remaining stands of old growth timber in the entire nation.

Forgotten were the cautionary tales going round before the war of timber ghost towns up in Washington. With a voyeuristic eye on the pent-up need for housing that would explode with war's end, the *Coos Bay Times* had rhapsodized in 1943, "If we're going to have full employment and full production . . . after the war, we're not going to make 'reserves' out of great resources of raw materials . . . we're going to look for even more."[1] Onward and upward, with chainsaws in our hands!

Production more than doubled at Coos Bay, in the war and early postwar years. Dozens of companies, big and small, created so many jobs that the area experienced a population boom. By 1947, if not earlier, Coos Bay was exporting more lumber than any other port in the Pacific Northwest. Other parts of the region had cut their private timber down by then, most of it anyway. But not Coos Bay. There a biggish company like Evans Products could anticipate "enough high-grade timber to run their Coos Bay operations indefinitely."[2] Evans added a plywood factory in 1948. Wisconsin-based Menasha Wooden Ware did the same, cashing in on some of its 56,000 acres of local timber. And so it went.

This was the economic context of the days and nights of my childhood. While Coos Bay's breadwinners were working shifts in local lumber mills and distant investors were making out like *banditos*, we were learning what a breeze it was to shoplift candy bars and sardine tins. We'd wolf our booty down in the security of the woods. If there were nothing else to do, we'd show up at the fountain of the Pay 'n Save to order water by the glass. Why the harried looking waitress went along with it is something I'll never know.

We were supposed to stay away from the busy industrial sites along the bay, which made them irresistible, of course. Especially attractive was a spot with open drums of tar. I was waving a big gob of it around on a stick one day when the head of a neighbor kid named Doug got in the way. Poor Doug. He went home screaming, and everybody knew where we had been.

We used to buy two or three newspapers as an excuse to board a foreign ship and go about its passageways. Any stray sailor who spotted our newspapers would offer us a handful of U.S. coins. It was a point of honor with us not to take much more than twice the paper's price.

The box factory was another place we weren't supposed to go. I remember weaving our bikes through narrow slots between the lumber stacks one day when suddenly, around a bend and bearing down on us, careened an empty lumber carrier. Ducking, we passed through its frame as if it were an open door. The driver smiled. We laughed. The war was done, and all of us were doing great. But one wrong move on the part of him or us and someone's head could have gone beneath the wheels of that carrier. It would not have been his.

In fact, it was around this time that Freddie Gum got run over by the trailer of a logging truck. The driver hadn't seen him on his bike. Having shown me up as a coward, Freddie Gum was not my friend. But I didn't want him killed.

Did anybody think back then that Coos Bay's economy could be run over by a logging truck? Given the kind of labor-saving technology that employers had adopted during the war—as leading example, the chainsaw—and continued strong demand for wood, a day of reckoning was bound to come around the bend, whether anybody thought so or not.

Coos Bay's postwar production frenzy was certain to attract some bigger fish to the pond, and sure enough it did, even though the milling capacity already in place exceeded annual timber growth. Weyerhaeuser Timber Company (Weyco), along with Menasha Wooden Ware and the C. A. Smith Lumber Company (which we'll get to know in Chapter 3) had acquired large amounts of virgin timber in the area in the first decade of the twentieth century. How they did this might be the subject of another book. Suffice it to say that Weyco got most of its acreage in a 1902 purchase of land at the headwaters of the Millicoma River, a tributary of the Coos. Consolidating dozens of additional acquisitions, Weyco put together a 210,000-acre reserve of old-growth timberland. Company foresters "mapped plans to convert [this] virtually undeveloped wilderness into a regulated forest which would yield a continuous supply of Douglas fir, cedar and hemlock logs."[3] Weyco was going to turn its forest into a log factory. But not yet, not yet.

Considering the extent of Weyco's Millicoma holdings and their economic potential for the area, Coos Bay residents had an important relationship with distant company executives of which most people were oblivious, I suspect. In 1951 Coos Bay's sleeping giant woke, opening a large new lumber plant at the south end of North Bend. At about the same time, the Army Corps of Engineers began dredging the Coos Bay bar and channel to permit the loading of large offshore ships. Coincidence? I doubt it. But Weyco's logging and manufacturing activities gave jobs to 500 people at the start. Over the next few years, the company would add other facilities, including a particle board plant, employ over 1000 Coos Bay area residents, and maintain a local payroll of nearly $5 million a year. To feed its mills, Weyco dumped the equivalent of 200 truckloads of logs into the Millicoma every twenty-four hours and towed them all to its factories on Coos Bay.

According to a knowledgeable source, Weyco began to liquidate its local timber holdings at a rate it "could have sustained . . . , if they had chosen to, forever."[4] Forever! And that was pretty much Weyco's stated intent. The company planned to replace logs from its old-growth timber "with a gradually increased amount taken from new growth [at its Millicoma Tree Farm, so that] [b]eginning about 1980, the yield from old-growth will diminish rapidly and the yield from new growth will be proportionately increased."[5]

The anticipated balance of death and rebirth was beautiful in its way, but nature was already accomplishing that. The problem for Weyco et al. was that nature didn't do it fast enough or in the volume that a factory forest might achieve. Using all the advances in forest management that we will run across in Chapter 12, Weyco would speed up the rhythm of nature to the advantage of . . . Coos Bay? I think we'd better keep an eye on Weyco's plan.

Five years later, in 1956, a second giant arrived on the scene when Georgia-Pacific Corporation (G-P) paid $70 million to take over Coos Bay Lumber Company, the area's largest employer and lumber producer prior to Weyco's start-up in North Bend. For its money, G-P got manufacturing plants, logging sites, transport links, and 120,000 acres of prime timberland. The timber was the biggest prize. Having arrived late at the plywood feast (a meal to be described in Chapter 10), this corporate behemoth needed timberland on its plate. Ever creative, G-P agreed to use future timber sales to finance a part of the deal for Coos Bay Lumber.

Paying for a timber purchase with the timber itself: it was such a brilliant stroke. But from the moment G-P's executives signed their names on the dotted line, the clock of compound interest was ticking on that timber that could buy itself. The clock was ticking, yet the company ran the following local ad: "The basis of Georgia-Pacific's entire forestry program is to ensure, over successive years, that we will grow a volume of timber at least equal to the volume harvested."[6]

Admiring the shining course of his company from the high ground of 1990, G-P Chair and CEO T. Marshall Hahn enthused that "...our story has been one of growth," and "the tree is the central character—the hero—of the Georgia-Pacific story."[7] But at Coos Bay G-P played the evil brother of Egyptian lore, cutting its hero into countless diverse parts until he disappeared. Why would G-P do a thing like that? The company's biographer had the answer on the tip of his pen: it was to "make as much money as possible for its stockholders."[8] Like any profit-taking corporation, that was what G-P lived for.

INVESTMENT in the processing and export of the Coos Bay area's prime resources did not begin with the arrival of Weyco and G-P. It had all the precedents to be discovered in Chapter 3 and more. Nor did corporate greed take off with World War II. The difference was the size of the domestic market, the technology for cutting timber, and the scale of the new investors' enterprises. G-P and Weyco were so big that they could use much of the area's timber to meet specialized internal needs, and they could afford to liquidate all of their Coos Bay timber within a few decades because they had so many other sources of supplies. With the appearance of these companies, the local economy became part of a new productive regime. This would eventually result in Coos Bay's disengagement from the flow of goods that circulates throughout the world, except to be, as minor retail outlet, one of the myriad end points in that flow. Thus would globalization come to Coos Bay.

ENDNOTES

1. Quoted in Robbins, *Hard Times* 104.

2. *Timberman* xlix.5 (March 1948): 100.

3. *The World*, May 15, 1961: 6B.

4. Quoted in Robbins, "The Social Context of Forestry: the Pacific Northwest in the Twentieth Century," *The Western Historical Quarterly* xvi (October 1985): 424.

5. Quoted in Emil R. Peterson and Alfred Powers, *A Century of Coos and Curry* (Portland: Binfords & Mort, 1952) 436.

6. *Coos Bay Times*, April 8,1959.

7. T. Marshall Hahn, *Georgia-Pacific Corporation: "The Growth Company"* (New York: Newcomen, 1990) 7.

8. John R. Ross, *Maverick: The Story of Georgia-Pacific* (place of publication unknown: G-P, 1980) 265.

CHAPTER 3

Pioneer Extractors

L IKE SOME of the other characters we're about to meet, my father had a lumberyard. His was at a windblown site in North Bend. I can still recall the general layout of the place, the smell of fresh-cut wood, the towering lumber stacks, the outhouse down the sandy slope behind the stacks, and one more thing. When I was about twelve years old, my dad decided I was ready to go to work for him. He put me behind the counter at the lumberyard. When a customer came in, I was supposed to wait on him, as if I knew anything about the lumberyard's supplies, prices, and policies. My dad's approach to on-the-job training was sink or swim. It was the shortest lasting job I ever had.

Despite stands of high-quality timber vast and near, the earliest builders at Coos Bay had no local source of wood supplies. They had to have their lumber shipped from San Francisco and Columbia River mills. Settlers cleared the land by setting fire to the woods. Eventually, no doubt, a sawmill would have taken care of local lumber needs, but Coos Bay's outlet to the sea, though not without considerable risks, suggested more ambitious schemes. Five years into the gold rush, the price of lumber in San Francisco was attracting lumber shipments from Maine, New Zealand, even Tasmania. If Coos Bay had wood to burn, Coos Bay had wood to sell. But the area's economic development required a bigger capitalist than any already there, someone with the wherewithal to build a sawmill and ship lumber to the soaring market down the coast.

Such a person soon appeared. Henry Heaton Luse hit the area in 1855, fresh from Yreka, a quintessential California gold boomtown. Five thousand men, one woman, and more than fifty saloons: that was what Yreka had. In this social wilderness, Luse had proven himself to be one of "the shrewd and calculating men [who got] into other business besides mining."[1] He had built a sawmill there. The proceeds from its sale proved enough for him to set up operations at Empire City, on the west leg of Coos Bay. But after building a steam-powered sawmill at that site, he had no money left for mill supplies. He had to fish drift logs out of the bay to have any wood to cut. For Luse, however, that was good enough to start, for what he lacked in capital he more than equalized in nerve and grit.

Besides the eighteen-hour days he worked (he required his men to work just twelve), Luse was thick-skinned. They could say what they wanted about the fact that he hired Chinese—Luse would have hired people from the moon if they would work for what he paid the Chinese! It wasn't long before he was not only exporting lumber but also operating a general store; manufacturing broom handles, lath, and matchwood; and monopolizing passenger traffic on the bay with two side-wheelers and a steam-driven tug. For settlers otherwise isolated by water and marshy, roadless land, the approach of Luse's *Alpha*, *Coos*, or *Satellite* to their piers must have seemed a welcome sight indeed.

Luse's career at Coos Bay crested with events that swirled around the "Warwick Donation," a hotly disputed property claim which might have made him, if not king of the hill, at least lord of the land on which was sprouting downtown Marshfield, the most dynamic commercial center in the area. Despite protracted litigation and the intervention by a U.S. senator on his behalf, it wasn't in a courtroom but in a muddy Marshfield street that things came to a head. Luse, a former surveyor himself, was leading the survey party he had hired when it approached an area occupied by E.B. Dean and Company's big new lumber mill. David Wilcox, a partner of E.B. Dean, confronted them there with a stick in his hand. Go ahead, Luse urged his crew. "Mr. Luse," said Wilcox, "[I]f you want them to go ahead take the chain and lead them yourself."[2] This Luse declined to do. He thought he had a better way of dealing with the situation than by getting his head bashed in. His subsequent lawsuit was thrown out on a demurrer, though, and downtown Marshfield (now Coos Bay) slipped from Luse's grasp.

As a fictional character, the area's first lumberman could have been a West Coast cousin of Flem Snopes and others of that Mississippi clan. But Luse clearly demonstrated how to succeed in lumbering at Coos

Bay. "When Luse sold out in 1882," says Stephen Dow Beckham, a Coos Bay historian, "the era of the local capitalist had ended."[3]

The second man to get a load of lumber over the Coos Bay bar had his office in San Francisco. He showed how to succeed in lumbering with a business empire. I refer to Asa Mead Simpson, whose sawmills at eight other locations in Oregon, Washington, and California; fleet of sailing ships and tugs; and lumberyards in Stockton, Sacramento, and San Francisco made him "king of the lumber coast" for 900 miles south from Puget Sound.[4] Simpson's Coos Bay operations, centered at the bay's northern bend (destined to become the north end of North Bend), especially the shipyard, were the jewel in the crown of this lumber king.

Son of a Maine shipbuilder and younger brother of shipbuilders, Simpson learned early on to build ships. Then, as he was learning to build even better ships, he heard a song from far off in the west: "If you trouble to come to me, I'm yours." Young Asa boarded one of his family's partly owned ships. He didn't put wax in his ears or order his crew to tie him to the mast. He and his brothers sailed south, following the sweet voice calling from the west around the horn of South America and up its Pacific coast, past Chile, Peru, and what remained of Mexico following the U. S.-Mexican War, until, in 1850, they arrived in San Francisco Bay, joining thousands of other men from all over the world who had also heard the siren song.

Simpson built a skiff and took it to the gold country. (That's so easy to say, but can you imagine building your own boat and then rowing and sailing it—for he must have been rowing when he wasn't sailing, just to hold his own against the current—and somehow getting it up the mighty Sacramento River more than a hundred miles to the mother lode?) There Simpson soon came up with $1,500 in gold, which he carried back to San Francisco, only to have some of it stolen from his room, some of it lost to a bad loan, and a bad investment flush the rest of it down the drain. Nothing for it but to take the remaining lumber from the voyage from Maine and turn it into a retail lumberyard, which promptly burned, of course. You can see the pattern here.

Simpson later prided himself on all the obstacles he had overcome en route to acquiring his title as the West Coast lumber king. His memoirs emphasize that getting knocked down and getting up again was this cat's game. As he put it, "indomitable perserverence [sic] will surmount all difficulties."[5] No doubt oblivious of the fact, Simpson was also one of those rare creatures so easily recognized on stage: a living, breathing stereotype. For example, he always wore a top hat, even to the logging camps. Once when swept off a slippery deck in a stormy sea, he devoted his efforts to retrieving his hat. A wave carried off both it and him—and they were surely lost. But no, another wave carried them back to the ship. Dripping but rehatted, Simpson clambered back on board without a word.

If "[a] hat in the ocean is the embrace of the unknown,"[6] Simpson also embraced what he possessed. He was so stingy that he refused to carry marine insurance, despite the loss of dozens of his ships. On the road, he even "blacked" his own shoes. When they called him "Stovepipe Simpson," it was only behind his back, for he had a terrible temper, too. At the age of eighty he attacked his North Bend shipbuilder's hull design with an ax. He had ordered something else, you see. Simpson hated the use of alcohol and banned its sale in his North Bend store. (Paternalistic? You bet, but would you rather work for an employer who conducts random tests for drugs?) For Simpson, business was the only permissible pleasure.

Except for one thing. Like Pygmalion, Simpson fell in love with his most beautiful creation, a clipper ship he called the *Western Shore*. She was perhaps "the fastest sailing ship of her time."[7] Fast and beautiful, that was she, except to the San Francisco snobs who turned their noses up at Simpson's masterpiece. They said she wasn't a clipper ship, at all. Simpson knew the criticism had to do with him, not her, and he could take it, too. What he couldn't take was having his beautiful vessel's bottom torn out on a reef outside the Golden Gate. It was dark, the captain of the *Western Shore* was drunk, and the passage was only a mile wide. This senseless loss broke Simpson's crusty heart.

I personally owe a debt of gratitude to the lumber king: the hundred acres of original forest which he preserved around the bend from his shipping and milling compound became, as Simpson Park, my childhood's playscape and memory map.

While Simpson's powerful integration of lumber manufacturing and shipping with his California sales outlets upped the capital requirements for successful West Coast lumbering, it did not allow him to dominate the industry at Coos Bay. He had competitors in Luse;

31

E.B. Dean; the mysterious Southern Oregon Improvement Company (SOIC), also known as. the Oregon Improvement Co. (OIC) and the Southern Oregon Co. (SOC), whose eastern backers bought out Luse and built a lumber manufacturing plant with the capacity to produce far more lumber than their California dealers could profitably sell; and others too. They all had their own ships and California market links. The key was having tugs for pulling cargoes cross the dangerous Coos Bay bar and out to sea.

In fact, these various firms refused the use of their tugs to one late-coming lumberman, offering Aaron Lobree $300 a month to shut his operation down, which he refused. But when Lobree died soon after of "congestion of the brain," Captain Simpson offered mourners the use of his tug.[8] As someone said, "There is no more rushing, pushing business than the manufacture of lumber."[9]

Lobree's widow (first name unknown) could push with the best of them. She made enough money running her late husband's operations to buy herself a farm, offer regular paydays to her men (a local first), increase the mill's capacity, and then to sell the lot to E.B. Dean, which promptly moved its Marshfield production to the Lobree plant.

WHILE I'M NOT GOING to discuss every lumber manufacturer who set up shop at Coos Bay before Weyerhaeuser Timber and Georgia-Pacific opened operations there, I do have to include Charles Axel Smith. A capable Swede, Smith immigrated to the United States in 1867, at the age of fourteen. Working part-time in a Minnesota hardware store, he caught the eye of the owner, John S. Pillsbury, governor of the state and a member of the flour milling family. The association took Smith into lumbering, which led to bigger and bigger things, until he had built an innovative plant in Minneapolis which may have cut more lumber than any other sawmill in the world.

But by then a considerable portion of the Great Lakes' forests of white pine that hadn't already been turned into shingles, framing, siding, and the like was on display in the Chicago lumber district, in thousands of lumber stacks. By 1900, lumber barons like Smith were casting about for a new frontier—a new source of timber, that is. There wasn't much remaining in the Great Lakes region, and the Southern pine was gone. Where to go next? How about the Pacific Northwest?

Smith assured himself of access to raw materials by illegally buy-

32

ing them up, grabbing thousands of acres of prime timber in south-western Oregon and the California redwood country. He didn't pioneer the use of dummy "entrymen," but he did give the practice a unique twist. The genial Swede paid Midwestern schoolteachers to come to Oregon for their summer vacations. All they had to give him in return was a homestead claim to timber acreage. Just put it in their name and give the deed to Mr. Smith. We may imagine the conscientious teacher worrying if it were really all right, what they were doing, and Smith's bland assurance that it was done all the time, much like attending church.

Named in Stephen Puter's *Looters of the Public Domain* as "*the* most flagrant violator of federal land laws" (my emphasis), Smith tried to buy and destroy every copy of the muckraking classic. But maybe Puter's charge was unfair. As Smith's contemporary Lincoln Steffens pointed out, "Our economic system, which held up riches, power, and acclaim as prizes to men bold enough and able enough to buy corruptly timber, mines, oil fields, and franchises and 'get away with it' was at fault."[10]

Entering Coos Bay like a cat in the night, Smith bought up E.B. Dean Lumber Company's logging and lumbering properties before people knew what was going on. This gave him 100,000 acres of timber in the area. His so-called Big Mill opened just south of Marshfield in 1908. The name says less than everything, for the Big Mill was a marvel of labor-saving and waste-conserving technology. Nevertheless, most of the logs processed there were only roughly cut and sent by company steamer to Smith's San Francisco-area facilities for most of the value-added work. That was where the big profits came in. Smith's predecessor, E.B. Dean, had done the same.

By 1922 Smith's company, reorganized in the preceding decade at the expense of 1,200 workers when its founder nearly drowned in debt, provided almost one-third of manufacturing employment in Coos County. The Big Mill's cut of 340,000 feet of lumber in an eight-hour shift approached the combined capacity of all of Asa Simpson's mills of half a century earlier. Editors of a leading trade journal thought that by adding logging camps, extending logging rail lines, and tunneling through a pesky mountain, the Coos Bay Lumber Company (as it was now called) would have an "almost unlimited timber supply."[11]

Smith's company survived both its founder's death in 1925 and a federal price-fixing complaint of 1941 to continue as the area's largest employer until 1951, when Weyerhaeuser Timber (also named in the federal suit) opened *its* big mill. This was the company that Georgia-Pacific bought in 1956 for $70 million.

IT WASN'T ONLY LUMBER that Coos Bay exported to the world's markets. There was also canned salmon. More important for the local economy, there was coal. The pioneer developers of the Coos Bay Commercial Company who made the arduous overland trek from Jacksonville, the gold boomtown about a hundred miles to the southeast, practically tripped over the stuff. (These men make a further appearance in Chapter 6.)

Coal mining had its one successful local capitalist, as lumbering had its Luse. Patrick Flanagan was a pioneer who got there first. When a detachment of Indian-fighting soldiers found themselves stranded on Coos Bay's North Spit in 1852, Flanagan brought them goods from his inland outpost on the Umpqua River twenty miles to the north. I imagine he was there a few months later when the *Nassau*, the first ship known to enter what was quickly publicized as a "new bay," came to pick up what was left of the soldiers' stores, as he would no doubt want to bid for any items he could offer in his store.

He *was* there the following year when the second ship to enter Coos Bay got inside the bar and couldn't sail out again. Peering across the misty estuary, crew members were alarmed by the approach of Indians in a canoe. As the craft neared their ship, they must have rubbed their eyes in disbelief. Their captain's orders might have gone like this: "Hold your fire, boys, don't shoot! There's a white man in there with the Indians!" It was Flanagan, of course.

He had liked Coos Bay so much he moved there after the soldiers marched off over the Seven Devils to Fort Orford down the coast. When the Jacksonville bunch discovered coal, Flanagan began to keep an eye out for it too. It wasn't long before his vigilance paid off. He and a partner developed the area's richest vein of coal, using the proceeds to open two stores. He devised simple but brilliant expedients for ventilating his mine and moving cars inside it. Selling out to California capitalists in 1884, Flanagan had a San Francisco-style mansion built by San Francisco carpenters.

As for his contemporaries in the Coos Bay mines, no doubt they worked hard, but they couldn't afford the cost of mining, shipping, and marketing coal. One by one they went to work for California companies. When Asa Simpson first arrived at Coos Bay in 1855, he didn't come to manufacture lumber but to export coal. The problem for him as the captain of a sailing ship was that when his hold was full of coal, he had to counterbalance it with something else on deck. What could Simpson use for a deck load? Coos Bay's surrounding stands of Douglas fir, red and white cedar, western hemlock, and Sitka spruce answered that.

In addition to the coal in the area's hills and ravines, men discovered gold right on the beach near the mouth of the Coquille River south of Coos Bay. If there had been as much gold as there was coal, or if Coos Bay's coal had been of better quality, mining companies might have done to local forests what they did to the Sierra Nevada's.[12] Powered by the Coquille, the area's first sawmill served the lumber needs of gold miners.[13]

Gradually, the gold played out. As for the coal, pouring capital down a hole in the ground was no guarantee of success. Many mining boomtowns turned to mining ghost towns. But over the years Coos Bay's coal industry provided thousands of jobs. It also helped addict the area to resource extraction as the basis of the local economy. As to the nature of the work the miners did, read chapter 2 of George Orwell's *The Road to Wigan Pier*, where you can follow him into the pit when the miners are at work, creeping for a mile or so through low and narrow passages, scraping your back at almost every step until you come to the coal seam being worked. Watch men shoveling coal while on their knees; marvel at the human capacity to adapt to such conditions; and choke on the dust. But bear in mind that the technology in Orwell's day was much better than the technology with which the Coos Bay miners must have worked.

I have to interject, this coal mining was news to me. The only mine I knew of as a North Bend boy was the "clay mine," mentioned earlier. This was actually a small, dripping cavity under the bridge, where our unwitting hands would sculpt clammy linga with the cold gray stuff of its floor and walls.

Coos Bay's coal never did run out. Consumers switched to fuel oil in the 1920s and one by one the mines shut down. Someday, when the price of coal gets high enough, one of the big oil companies that have bought up most of the nation's coal reserves may reopen mining operations at Coos Bay. Energy politics being what they are, such a day could be near.[14] A note to would-be miners though: don't hold your breath. But isn't it ironic? At Coos Bay they have depletion of the resource that supposedly renews itself ("Timber is a Crop"), while coal, a non-renewable resource, remains in the ground.

ENDNOTES

1. Henry Kent, miner, quoted in Robert V. Hine and John M. Faragher, *The American West: A New Interpretative History* (New Haven: Yale University Press, 2000) 238.

2. Quoted in Orvil Dodge, *Pioneer History of Coos and Curry Counties, Or.* (Salem: Capital Printing, 1898) 165.

3. Stephen Dow Beckham, *Coos Bay: The Pioneer Period* (Coos Bay: Arago Books, 1973) 31.

4. See Thomas R. Cox, "Lumber and Ships: the Business Empire of Asa Mead Simpson," *Forest History* 14.2 (July 1970) 17.

5. Dictation to D.R. Sessions, July 7, 1891, 37. Courtesy of the Bancroft Library, University of California, Berkeley.

6. Michael Vandelaar and Tim White, "Trouble in Mind or, Dead Fish Never Grow Old," *Arsenal: Surrealist Subversion,* ed. Franklin Rosemont (Chicago: Black Swan, 1989) 134.

7. Peterson and Powers 502.

8. *Coos Bay News*, March 15, 1882; May 17, 1882.

9. M.L. Saley, quoted in Robbins, *Lumberjacks and Legislators: Political Economy of the U.S. Lumber Industry, 1890–1941* (College Station, TX: Texas A&M University Press, 1982) 30.

10. Quoted in Gray Brechin, *Imperial San Francisco: Urban Power, Earthly Ruin* (Berkeley: University of California Press, 1999) 190.

11. *The Timberman* xxiii.10 (August 1922): 57.

12. Cf. Brechin.

13. Factual material as to mining in the area obtained mostly from Beckham, *Coos Bay*, and Nathan Douthit, *The Coos Bay Region 1890–1944*: Life on a Coastal Frontier (Coos Bay: River West Books, 1981).

14. In 2001, with the Bush administration boosting coal-fired power plants in response to California's energy crisis and with the U.S. withdrawing from the Kyoto Protocol, the price of U.S. coal doubled in six months. *New York Times Magazine, July 22,* 2001, pp. 31-34.

CHAPTER 4

Another Queen?

BRILLIANT PROSPECTS attended the original white settlement of Coos Bay. An inland merchant thought it "second only to San Francisco" as an entrepôt.[1] Louis J. Simpson, Asa's son, went even further, discovering in Coos Bay an embryo of San Francisco. An embryonic San Francisco? Handsome Louie was a Coos Bay booster ... but why not? Like others of his generation, Simpson must have been impressed with the fact that San Francisco, not so long before, had been a sleepy outpost on the far-off California coast. The Yankee hide dealers who risked life, limb, and ship to sail around Cape Horn would put in there. For everyone else, San Francisco was little more than a rumor of a godforsaken place with exceptional harborage. Henry Dana's *Two Years Before the Mast* provides a fascinating, first-hand account.

If California were to be developed, San Francisco and its magnificent harbor would become "the centre of its prosperity." Dana could see that.[2] But before reports of California gold reached Washington, kindling the campaigns of plunder known as the Mexican-American war,[3] there was no good reason to believe that California *would* be developed any time soon. Most immigrants coming west headed for the lush valleys of Oregon, not south to arid California.

So, no gold, no booming San Francisco soon. But gold *was* discovered, even before John Sutter set about constructing his famous lumber mill. Coos Bay's timber, coal, and salmon, and the rich soil of its bottoms, were pay dirt of a different kind, sufficiently valued to attract settlements of farmers, workers, fishermen, and townsfolk, but not likely to draw enough of them to make up a city.

San Francisco enjoyed not only historical but also geographic advantages over Coos Bay and every other port along the coast. It was not just that the estuary known as San Francisco Bay is many times larger than the estuary known as Coos Bay. San Francisco was superbly accessible to every Pacific port, whereas Coos Bay, boxed in by rugged hills, was only accessible via a treacherous bar. More importantly, San Francisco Bay is the only harbor along the California coast providing natural access to the great Central Valley running parallel with the coast. The rivers flowing into San Francisco Bay also provide conveyance *within* the Valley, both north and south, which is why Asa Simpson built himself a skiff as soon as he reached land.

Conversely, the fingers of Coos Bay's sloughs and Coos River's meandering forks gave access to great stands of timber and to deposits of coal, but not to the gold country or rich farmland of Oregon's interior. Why? Because they flow from watersheds within the Coast Range. If we can join Anne Michaels in seeing "every river [as] a tongue of commerce, finding first geological then economic weakness and persuading itself,into continents,"[4] we must conclude that the tongue of Coos Bay's commerce didn't penetrate very far.

But enough of risqué metaphors. Let's look at some specifics of San Francisco's Topsy-like growth.

Because of the gold miners' dependence on imported food, San Francisco became an entrepôt where men unloaded cargoes of supplies bound for the gold towns in the Sierra foothills, carting the goods to warehouses or loading them directly onto river boats. The merchants would usually want to store such goods until they could get a decent price, meaning a highly exorbitant price from the point of view of hungry forty-niners. Amsterdam merchants had done the same, collecting, storing, selling, and reselling "the goods of the universe."[5] Venice and Antwerp had also followed that course. With the stockpiling of goods at one place, the merchant sets the price. He and others of his class grow powerful and rich enough to keep an ear out for investment opportunities elsewhere in the region.

Not long after the discovery of gold at Sutter's half-built mill, so much of it flowed into the former Yerba Buena that "San Francisco had money to burn . . . ."[6] Some people did anyway. But though it frequently changed hands, the money did not burn. An English adventurer who landed there in 1850 observed that the brick buildings lining Montgomery Street were the only structures left standing by a fire that destroyed everything else. These buildings housed the banks, so their cellars were fireproof. Mining wealth produced finance capitalists, whose subordination to eastern financiers was buried in silver by the

Comstock Lode. At the end of the nineteenth century, more than twice as much wealth passed through San Francisco banks than those of Seattle, Portland, Salt Lake City, and Los Angeles combined. San Francisco money made southern California.

The so-called Queen City of the West also manufactured the equipment used by western miners, as well as those of Australia and South America. San Franciscans manufactured farm and mill machinery. When Central Valley growers switched from wheat to barley, fruit, rice, and vegetables, what poured into San Francisco as produce left town as canned and packaged goods. The city had the largest fruit and vegetable cannery in the world.

Pacific Northwest flour millers had to transship their goods through San Francisco until the 1880s. Such was the Queen's dominance of maritime commerce. I could write more about oil from the Central Valley; the world's largest oil refinery across the bay in nearby Richmond; the city's cargo trade with China, Japan, the Philippines, and many other areas. But it all gets to be too much. Henry George called it "*the* city, . . . New York, Boston, Portland, Philadelphia, Richmond and Charleston . . . rolled into one."[7] Surely one decent city is enough!

But just to drive home the point, by the end of the 1860s, San Francisco was the center of an economic empire extending from Alaska to Panama, and from Hawaii to beyond the Rockies. Accidents of history and geography had given San Francisco an exceptional edge, precluding the growth of competitors until the transcontinental railroads hooked the West Coast to the national economy and allowed the take-off of Seattle, Portland, and Los Angeles. As the great historian Braudel put it, "In the economic poker game, some people have always held better cards than others, not to say aces up their sleeves."[8]

One of the aces dealt in recent centuries is the market system itself, which tends to accentuate early advantages. As Gunnar Myrdal said, "economic development is a process of circular and cumulative causation which tends to award its favours to those who are already well endowed and even to thwart the efforts of those who happen to live in regions that are lagging behind."[9]

If Coos Bay didn't have the makings of another San Francisco, what could it be? Well, some San Francisco capitalists dropped surplus earnings into Coos Bay's coal mines, as we have seen. Coos Bay's canned salmon got transshipped from the Queen City's piers. Coos

Bay's lumber manufacturing merchants, such as Luse and Simpson, stocked their stores with goods from there. More importantly for Coos Bay, San Francisco became both the "main West Coast market for lumber and the nerve center from which its manufacture was increasingly controlled."[10] Operations at Coos Bay, with their integration of local manufacture, maritime transport, and California retail outlets were duplicated from Santa Cruz on north along the coast, wherever waterways gave access to marketable timber stands. San Francisco capital built and controlled all the larger operations. Asa Simpson and the other giants of this early cargo trade "stood with one foot in San Francisco and the other at the point of production."[11] One point of production was Coos Bay.

San Francisco's lumber imperium lasted until the end of the nineteenth century, when the intercontinental rail links spurred building spurts in Portland and Seattle, and Great Lakes' capital began to meet the region's financial needs. For lumber manufacturers, San Francisco then became "a place to ship one's excess cut or grades not in demand elsewhere."[12] More importantly, government sponsorship of intercontinental railroads and (in its start-up phase) telegraphy, along with corporate reorganization and consolidation of key industries, pulled all of the country's regional economies together into a national network.[13] A similar process would occur in the latter half of the twentieth century when advances in communications technology, corporate mergers, and the hitching of state power to the dynamo of business imperatives would combine to build a global economy.[14] With that would come a shakeout of the economic order that would leave many formerly vital communities like Coos Bay, many regions of the world, and at least one continent, far, far removed from the major flows of investment and trade.

For Coos Bay, rail linkage to the national economy remained a dream deferred well into the new century. Thus, the area continued to court the aging Queen long after other Pacific Northwest sites had found markets for their products in the nearest regional powerhouse. Between 1900 and World War I, San Francisco imported more lumber from Coos Bay than from any other Pacific Northwest port.

INSTEAD OF BECOMING *another* San Francisco, Coos Bay became a *dependency* of San Francisco, so joined to the city by the Golden Gate that Oregon's leading newspaper described it as "a part of

California."[15] Coos Bay residents looked to San Francisco merchants for whatever they couldn't make for themselves at home, so that, for example, a woman might sew her family's clothes, but "[a]ll the material, buttons, and shoes were ordered from San Francisco."[16]

People who *could* didn't order buttons from a catalogue but took passage on a coal company ship to go to San Francisco to shop. They also shipped their children off to school there. Luse went there to die. Flanagan had his San Francisco-style house. The point is clear: the California center's dominance was both economic and a thing of the mind.

When you come right down to it, Coos Bay could not become another San Francisco because there already *was* a San Francisco. For the first sixty or so years of history following the white takeover I discuss in Chapter 6, Coos Bay was a minor appendage of the city by the Golden Gate, which does not, of course, make the people who lived at Coos Bay any less valuable or beautiful as human beings, but it does go far, I think, toward explaining why there were so many more such valuable, beautiful people making their lives in one location rather than the other.

In thinking that Coos Bay would be a San Francisco of the north, the pioneering boosters misjudged the area's situation grievously—or hoped that others would. Coos Bay had natural riches, yes. But for fully realized economic development, such natural wealth is never enough. Otherwise, the hungry people of Congo (the former Zaire) might enjoy the highest living standards in the world today, instead of having been born into a country "too rich for her own good," a princess of a country colonized and robbed blind.[17]

Coos Bay's "unexcelled" timber and exceptional harbor were a magnet for remotely based investors, which meant that the area's natural wealth got sucked into the accounts of people who might never visit Coos Bay. Their stake was in extracted wealth, not local residents. This means that people at Coos Bay have unacknowledged cousins in colonized areas of the Third World, places where "the greater the wealth available for exploitation, the poorer and more undeveloped the region today."[18]

But the alert and clever reader might question this. It wasn't like Caesar requisitioning grain from the Gauls: Coos Bay wasn't simply robbed. Surely Coos Bay got something of roughly equal value for its exported wealth. Well, no. Not to put too fine a point on it, but outside the schoolyard (a site already notorious for bullies) trade doesn't usually mean equal exchange. As the academic writer Richard Peet notes, "The geography of trade is a massive spatial process of wealth transfer: trade does not equalize, but instead concentrates wealth."[19] The consequences are well known: "whenever a lot of money comes together in just one hand it's always a kind of robbery of the rest of us."[20]

Typically, trade involves "asymmetrical exchange" between a core area, such as nineteenth-century San Francisco, and a peripheral supply region. With the closure of its mills, Coos Bay has even fallen out of the periphery on which the centers of wealth and power feed—as giant leeches on a living corpse? Had my family remained in North Bend I doubt that I would find those words too strong.

Anyway, most of Coos Bay's exports did not go directly to markets. They went to the exporting firms' sales outlets or to one of its other production units. Whether it was Simpson's lumber cargoes or the output of G-P's formaldehyde plant, products mainly left Coos Bay as intrafirm transfers. G-P, again, might send Coos Bay-manufactured chemicals to another G-P site in the Pacific Northwest for use in manufacturing there; might send plywood from its Coos Bay plywood operation to one of its dozens of "one-step" distribution centers somewhere in the United States; might ship white cedar logs to its agents in Japan. As the companies leading executives said in 1966, "each component of our organization tends to further the growth of some other component."[21] So, it wasn't really trade at all.

Whether San Francisco was *the* city or a city, Coos Bay's major producers did not look to local needs to determine what to produce and whether it might make sense, financially, to discontinue production for a few weeks to let the market take up slack. They looked to their firms' requirements. And Coos Bay was ripe for plunder from its start.

But an issue remains. What happened to the spatial dimension of Coos Bay's dependency when San Francisco lost its empire? Among the companies that came to dominate the local economy in the mid-twentieth century, Weyerhaeuser was headquartered in a suburb of Tacoma, Washington; Georgia-Pacific in Portland, Oregon; and Menasha Corporation in Wisconsin. Some argue that, with corporate hegemony, economic power has lost its territorial center. But that's another book.[22] As for San Francisco, that bay area has become a node in a system of global flows of capital, goods, and services.

Consequently, its linkages to other global centers far outweigh its links to what were once its hinterlands.[23]

ENDNOTES

1. Quoted in Beckham, *Coos Bay* 10.

2. Richard Henry Dana, Jr., *Two Years Before the Mast* (Hertfordshire, England: Wordsworth Ed., 1996) 187.

3. Cf. Brechin 29-30.

4. Anne Michaels, *Fugitive Pieces* (New York: Vintage, 1998) 26.

5. Fernand Braudel, *The Perspective of the World*, trans. Sian Reynolds (New York: Perenial Library, 1986) 236-37.

6. James E. Vance, Jr., *Geography and Urban Evolution in the San Francisco Bay Area* (Berkeley: Universitiy of California Institute for Governmental Studies, 1964) 13.

7. Quoted in Gunther Barth, *Instant Cities: Urbanization and the Rise of San Francisco and Denver* (New York: Oxford University Press, 1975) 219.

8. Braudel 48.

9. Gunnar Myrdal, *Development and Underdevelopment: A Note on the Mechanism of National and International Economic Inequality* (Cairo: National Bank of Egypt, 1956) 47.

10. Thomas Cox, *Mills and Markets: A History of the Pacific Coast Lumber Industry to 1900* (Seattle: University of Washington, 1974) 71. Reprinted by permission of the University of Washington Press.

11. Cox, *Mills and Markets* 137. Reprinted by permission of the University of Washington Press.

12. Cox, *Mills and Markets* 285. Reprinted by permission of the University of Washington Press.

13 Alfred D. Chandler, Jr., *The Visible Hand: The Managerial Revolution in American Business* (Cambridge, Mass.: Belknap, 1977).

14. Cf. William K. Tabb, *The Amoral Elephant: Globalization and the Struggle for Social Justice in the Twenty-First Century* (New York: Monthly Review Press, 2001).

15. Quoted in Robbins, *Hard Times* 17.

16. Douthit, *Coos Bay Region* 60.

17. Barbara Kingsolver, *The Poisonwood Bible* (New York: Harper, 1998) 456.

18. André Gunder Frank, *Lumpenbourgeoisie: Lumpendevelopment: Dependence, Class, and Politics in Latin America*, trans. Marion D. Berdecio (New York: Monthly Review Press, 1972) 19.

19. Richard Peet with Elaine Hartwick, *Theories of Development* (New York: The Guilford Press, 1999) 10. Cf. Joan Robinson, *Aspects of Development and Underdevelopment* (New York: Cambridge University Press, 1979) 102ff.

20. Miguel Ángel Asturias, *Men of Maize*, trans. Gerald Martin (Pittsburgh: University of Pittsburgh Press, 1993) 297.

21. Owen Cheatham and Robert B. Pamplin, *The Georgia-Pacific Story* (New York: The Newcomen Society, 1966) 18.

22. See, e.g., Hardt and Negri, *Empire* (Cambridge, Mass.: Harvard University Press, 2000).

23. See Manuel Castells, *The Rise of the Network Society* (Cambridge, Mass.: Blackwell Publishers, 1996) 386.

CHAPTER 5

Pirates at the Bar

OWARD THE END of the nineteenth century, when Coos Bay began to enter the competition to become the "lumber capital of the world,"[1] an observer of the region might have warned the area's residents of the hazards of grafting their economy to lumber exports. For one thing, with depletion of the Port Orford cedar in the twentieth century (discussed in Chapter 12), Coos Bay's growing specialization in wood product exports would be no different than that of any place else in the Douglas fir region of the Pacific Northwest. In other words, Coos Bay's economy wasn't specialized, just narrowly based.

Secondly, although huge corporations have come to dominate the industry, the bulkiness of logs traditionally favored a mushrooming of small producers. Thus, the industry as a whole had a tendency to produce too much. From the viewpoint of investors, there was a chronic problem of overcapacity. What did it matter if the many saws of SOIC (the company that bought out Luse) could turn out 120,000 feet of lumber a day if the company could not profitably sell even half that amount? On the other hand, if lumber had not been easier to ship than logs, Coos Bay might not have gotten the industry it did. But more on this below.

Another problem with lumber industrialization (or another way of looking at the same problem) was its dependence on the ups and downs of distant markets, over which producers lacked control. In 1882, when SOIC's investors were discovering the "unexcelled" quality of Coos Bay's timber, the number of ships crossing the local bar was mainly limited by the availability of tugs. The industry boomed. Four years later, with the California market saturated, Coos Bay's mills were shutting down. Within another year the local news source had pronounced the area's lumber industry "dead."[2]

Coos Bay's boosters regarded the area's timber as "inexhaustible,"[3] despite surging investment in mechanizing and powering up the manufacture of lumber and a series of logistical innovations that allowed access to more and more trees. When they could no longer use the force of gravity to slide logs down the hills and into the estuary, loggers employed ox teams and skid roads; freshets, flumes, and tramways; splash dams and locomotives, whatever it took to get logs in the water and headed in the direction of the mills. "If we had the market to supply," thought Asa Simpson toward the end of his long career, "the output could be doubled at a day's warning."[4] Warning? To whom? Surely not to the trees. But we get his drift. *The inexhaustibility of Coos Bay's forests required tepid demand.*

Simpson guessed that the Pacific Coast's supply of timber was "sufficient for 3 or 4 generations." By the time it ran out, "they will have discovered a substitute for timber"—or replanted trees.[5] Many wood substitutes *have* been found. And "they" have replanted plenty of trees. But an adequate substitute for lumber mill employment at places like Coos Bay has yet to be found, while a substitute for native forests rendered into wood products has yet to come to mind.

Private financing of the area's development served the needs of the investors, not those of local communities. Consider Coos Bay's infra-structure—roads, bridges, rail links, etc. For decades, railroad spurs brought logs to Coos Bay's mills and coal to the bunkers at the bay, while the only way for a traveler to get from North Bend to Marshfield, a mere three miles away, was by boat. (Luse's monopoly on maritime passenger traffic was no small thing.) Both as consumers and producers, residents of Coos Bay and other southwestern Oregon sites had better connections to San Francisco than to one another. For example, in 1885 it was cheaper for Bandon potato growers to send their produce to San Francisco than to Coos Bay, twenty-five miles up the coast.[6]

Traveling to and from the area was often downright dangerous. Nathan Douthit describes an incident from 1907 that might have warmed the canvas of a Géricault or Delacroix: a stagecoach capsized in the surf, the passengers struggling "to keep their heads above sand and water," and the loosened horses dashing down the beach. Rescuers took turns carrying a fur-wrapped girl whom a wave had nearly stolen from her mother's arms.[7] When the area finally did get some roads, they seemed modeled on corduroy.

Coos Bay was like colonial Africa, where the roads "led to the seaports and the sea lanes led to Western Europe and North America."[8] San Francisco was Coos Bay's Western Europe and North America. It took the desperation of the Depression, when New Deal funding helped build McCullough Bridge, for Marshfield and North Bend to gain a surface link to Portland and the coastal north. Residents of my father's generation and earlier had had to cross the estuary by ferry for such a trip.

No wonder Coos County's roads were so bad they made me sick. The nausea was one thing; the humiliation . . . but I'll save the details for my therapist. I didn't recognize progress when it was hitting me in the gut. The six-hour drive to Portland in my father's truck was a journey measurable in days not many decades earlier. Six hours seemed an eternity to me. When we finally got to the city, though, how exciting it all was: the hustle-bustle, the urban grit, the smell of roasting coffee, and the nighttime riot of neon lights. Speaking of ads, all over town were giant come-ons for the latest out of Hollywood, "The Outlaw," evidently starring Jane Russell's breasts.

Unlike the WPA project that gave Coos Bay its bridge, most federal help served shippers' needs, by trying to stabilize the area's treacherous artery to the sea. I've mentioned Coos Bay's dangerous bar and alluded to the fact (in Chapter 3) that a shipwreck led to settlement of the area by whites. The entrance to Coos Bay was both an invitation and a trap. By 1928, when federally funded dredging and jetty-building efforts began to pay off, enough ships had run aground on the bar to allow people—some people anyway—to make a living from scavenged shipwrecked goods. These people were disparaged as the "South Slough Pirates."

But people who were either too lazy or too clever to hold a job were not the only pirates at Coos Bay. In November 1915 the *Santa Clara*, with ninety-one people and 400 tons of Christmas-sale merchandise on board, lost the use of her steering gear and ran aground on the bar's south spit. She then lay a short distance offshore with water pouring through a gaping wound in her hull. Thinking she was about to break up, the captain chose to launch the lifeboats. The first boat that attempted to cross the roiling patch of sea between the ship and shore had the women and children on board. ("Women and children first!") It promptly overturned. Seventeen of its occupants were lost. Recovered bodies were stacked in a beachfront shack. Those people died unnecessarily, it seems, because the ship did not break up.

When people understood that the *Santa Clara* would not easily go down, tragedy turned to farce. Hundreds of Coos Bay residents, including Marshfield businessmen with merchandise on board the ship, gathered at the site to involve themselves in what soon degenerated into a "mad orgy" of looting over the next several days. Some people even swam the deadly gap between the shore and stricken ship.

"Had the *Santa Clara* and her cargo been lost in the wildest part of the world," the *Coos Bay Times* editorialized, "the owners of the goods aboard would have had no less protection than they did within half a mile of the entrance of Coos Bay."[9] Or, as another local writer quipped, the "only way you could tell a Marshfield pirate from a South Slough pirate was by the superior strategy he [the Marshfield native, presumably] showed in getting away with the flotsam."[10]

With the *Santa Clara*'s foundering, "plunder" became the area's secret middle name. And when Marshfield named itself Coos Bay in 1944, it seemed to North Bend boys another act of piracy: why should Marshfield get the name of the bay? We refused to utter the rival town's new name for years. But most other people did.

So much of Coos Bay's pioneer history centered on a place a few miles north of the Coos Bay bar. I mean Empire—or, as it was called in the early years, Empire City. *Our* Empire was a rather down-at-heel place we had to drive through on the way to my aunt's. Approaching it, we got a whiff of smoked salmon and tidal flats. Soon came Empire's chowder stands, white houses with peeling paint, faded blue hydrangeas, and glimpses of the bay through trees. We might have seen the North Spit on the other side, if somebody had pointed it out. The story of the North Spit castaways, the soldiers who got stranded there in 1852, would have had us listening up.

"There's the Seven Devils Road," my father would always say, as we passed a lonely turnoff south of Empire. If he knew that the Seven Devils was the rugged route taken out of the area by the castaways when their commanding officer finally arrived, he kept it to himself. Nor did my father say anything about Jedediah Smith having come that way in 1828 or mention the places that we knew, such as Sunset Beach, where the Smith party had camped. Our teachers were mum on this, as well. Thus, the local geography had no history for us; the Seven

Devils was just a road with a slightly scary name that we never had to take, thank God.

The only thing of interest in those parts was our Aunt Jean's place in Charleston, with its "windmill" (actually a wind-powered well), outhouse, and hard pinecones for flinging at one another until my little brother got hurt. Briefly flinging itself from wall to wall above our heads one evening came a bat, just as the radio was trumpeting Rossini's thrilling announcement of another episode of "The Lone Ranger," which for some reason we could only listen to at my aunt's. For a special treat, we might venture out to sea on Uncle Clyde's fishing boat.

Empire was well on the periphery of our little world. At its center was the rivalry between the North Bend Bulldogs and the Marshfield Pirates. I still recall the excitement, soon after we moved to North Bend, of going to the high school practice field to watch much bigger boys colliding with a thud and a little puff of dust. North Bend and Marshfield were rivals in everything that mattered, meaning school sports. If Saturday night came with the Bulldogs playing basketball at home, oh wow! That high school gym would be jammed with screaming, sweating North Bend fans. There was no television, after all, no local college team. High school football and basketball, experienced fresh and raw, was as good as it got around there. Without Bulldog football and basketball, our falls and winters would have consisted entirely of rain and frost.

We lived and died with those teams, including even the Baby Bulldogs of Roosevelt Junior High. In the end, we usually died, because in the big showdown with Marshfield teams, the Pirates usually managed to steal a win. At least it seemed like theft to us. You could even say that local sports prepared me for a life in which the good guys never seemed to win. But there, in that gym on a Friday or Saturday night, with almost everybody we knew present and almost everybody longing for the same thing . . . well, it was a high I've never quite revisited. I never thought to wonder how the Marshfield Pirates might have come by their name.

I tried to visit Empire the last time I was in the Coos Bay area, but Coos Bay (the town) had gobbled Empire up some years before, and what had given it its Empirish quality was no longer there. Unconvinced, I headed south along the half-remembered road that goes along the estuary and its ragged line of woods, trying to sniff something out. It must have been high tide, as even the old smells were gone. The feeling that I used to get of being tucked inside a chowder stand was also gone. It was a mild day, however, and I took a lot of pictures at the Charleston harbor and the Coos Bay bar.

The entrance to the bay *looked* placid enough. I picked my way through driftwood and tall grass, remembering what I'd learned about the shipwrecks there. Over sixty ships have been lost in the vicinity. The only reason that the risky bar didn't put Coos Bay at a major disadvantage early on was that access to rival ports was just as hazardous or more. Economic development of the area made shipwrecks inevitable.

Sea lanes have remained the best way of transporting bulky goods to and from Coos Bay. But not all of Coos Bay's shipwrecks are moldering in the past. As recently as 1999, while I was poring over interesting documents in Berkeley's drafty libraries, the carcass of a Japanese tanker called the *New Carissa*, which had run aground some 150 yards offshore, was drifting north along the Oregon coast, turning up again and again like an obscene message on the face of the earth, threatening additional leakage of its 400,000 gallons of fuel oil at each new site.

ENDNOTES

1. Quoted in Robbins, *Hard Times* 107.

2. Cox, *Mills and Markets* 164, 191; *Coos Bay News*, June 30, 1886; May 4, 1887.

3. According to the *Coos Bay News* of February 29, 1888, "Our forests are practically inexhaustible for timber."

4. Simpson 1891, 15. Courtesy of the Bancroft Library, University of California, Berkeley.

5. Simpson 1891, 15. Courtesy of the Bancroft Library, University of California, Berkeley.

6. *Coos Bay News*, April 15, 1885.

7. Douthit 34-35.

8. Walter Rodney, *How Europe Underdeveloped Africa* (Washington, D.C.: Howard University Press, 1972) 230.

9. Quoted in Douthit 130.

10. Quoted in Douthit 130.

CHAPTER 6

Original Plundering

THE TAPROOT of Coos Bay's plundering reached down into the soil of Sutter's mill. Forty-niners and other latecomers to the gold bonanza dashed from one northern California boomtown to the next—Angels Camp, Murphys, Columbia, Sonora, Shasta City, Truckee, Yreka—until a few of them landed in southern Oregon where, sometime in the early winter of 1851-52, somebody found gold at a Rogue River valley site. By February, gold rushers had staked out the entirety of what they called Rich Gulch. A tent trading post supplied tools, rough clothing, tobacco, and whiskey. By March the settlement had its first log cabin, a forest of tents, additional traders, and a regular supply of hand-sawed, high-priced lumber. Gamblers, prostitutes, and "sharpers of every kind" brought diversity to the social milieu.[1] Called Jacksonville, the settlement was on its way to becoming southern Oregon's first town.

Following a winter when snow blocked supplies and Jacksonville's residents had to live on unsalted beef and game, dozens of new settlers arrived. Included in this mix was one Perry B. Marple, a former minister, who extolled the "beauties and advantages" of a certain Coos Bay. He found plenty of listeners, as "a perfect fever raged" to find a seaport through which Jacksonville could get its supplies.[2] Following the seventeenth-century model for international business success established by the Dutch, Marple organized a joint stock company, the Coos Bay Commercial Company, to go to Coos Bay "and take possession of the country."[3] The fact that there were already perhaps 2,000 indigenous people living in dozens of villages around the estuary and its sloughs was of no reported concern. Whites no longer saw a need by 1853 to invoke a God-given right to "unused" land, as had the Puritans in Massachusetts. It was simply understood. Marple owed his knowledge of Coos Bay to a visit there the previous year when he, six other whites, and a pair of Indian guides had gone from Winchester (just north of present-day Roseburg) to the Umpqua River settlement of Scottsburg, then down the river to its mouth and twenty miles south along the Pacific to Coos Bay. But Marple did not propose to duplicate this roundabout trip. Instead, he would do what few, if any, other whites had done, by taking the party over the rugged, untracked coastal range. No doubt he counted on hooking up with some navigable part of the Coquille River before they had gone very far. And he would charge the others $10,000 as a "piloting" fee, a requirement that Marple did not divulge until the trek was well under way. This disclosure may have been the cause of over half the members of the original forty or so turning back, or it may have been the steep and brushy route, though their horses must have done most of the work.

Fearing Indians, what was left of the Coos Bay Company eventually came to a fork in the Coquille where there were some Indians. The natives quickly disappeared into the woods, which is where they might have remained if one of them hadn't understood the language of the developers' guide. Attracted by the possibility of acquiring treasures, or what the whites thought of as trinkets, out they reluctantly came. After some discussion, a few of them agreed to take the whites down river in canoes. The whites indulged themselves by giving their porters ironic names, such as George Washington and King David. The Indians indulged *themselves* by stopping for a visit at every native village along the river's course. They probably got an additional laugh when the sleeping whites were swamped by the river's morning tide.

There were hundreds of people in one place where the travelers stayed. The whites communicated "the best they could with the shy and stoical redmen who ... looked upon [them] with astonishment as [if] they were a different type of humanity ..."[4] Their "astonishment" may have been terror, for the U. S. military had sent a punitive expedition up the Coquille River less than two years earlier. The fifteen Indians killed were probably relatives of these villagers.

W.H. Harris, whose journal has permitted our armchair participation in this trek from Jacksonville, had taken over leadership of the nineteen men who finally arrived at Coos Bay's South Slough. There they encountered "nearly nude" Indians harvesting salmon. Native villages lined the estuary's bank a little farther on. The scene was "romantic in the extreme."[5] Exchanges were negotiated, but "[t]he natives did not seem to appreciate the value of gold or silver coins." They had "shells which the Hudson Bay Co. had traded them for furs,"[6] valued according to their size.

Harris had a better eye than other journal keepers who encountered the Coosans in their native land. He noted that they were wild about the clothing of the pioneer developers. In fact, they "were eager to possess any article of clothing that they could...[for example, a] red shirt, or bandana handkerchief..."[7] This accorded with the experience of the North Spit castaways of the previous year. Then, in exchange for the fish, venison, geese, ducks, and elk meat brought them by a local chief and his "long packtrain of squaws," the soldiers offered hardtack, rice, tobacco, and clothes. It was the clothes that made their eyes light up, pleasing "them extremely well, especially the jackets, which were decorated with grand yellow lace and a multitude of brass buttons."[8]

What was it about whites' clothes that made them irresistible to Coos Bay's natives? My guess is that it was the unfamiliar colors. Take red, a color highly charged, no matter whether on a torso, flag, or tied to the end of a load of lumber on my father's truck. We see it everywhere, of course. Native youths, on the other hand, would go to tremendous lengths to obtain the "scalp" of a redheaded woodpecker, a very few of which might suffice to make the daughter of the richest chief one's bride. Where else did one find red in this environment? There was the color of blackberries on their way to ripening. Every child knew what that red meant. There was also the red of sunsets, but this was a fearsome thing, portending illness in children, perhaps because it was the color of blood. Obtainable, preservable red was rare, yet the whites wore it casually on their backs and round their necks.

Compare an African's account of his capture into slavery: "When the kings saw that the whites were taking out these scarlet handkerchiefs . . . they told the blacks, 'Go on then, go and get a scarlet handkerchief' and the blacks were so excited by the scarlet that they ran down to the ships like sheep and they were captured."[9]

But fascination with some item of the others' clothing was not limited to one side. The observant Harris noted that the females at South Slough wore "only . . . a rude apron ingeniously woven from sea weeds and cedar roots."[10]

In 1853, when members of the Coos Bay Commercial Company appeared in their midst, the area's natives had had sufficient prior contacts with whites that they had a name for them. They called them the "moving people." What they called themselves is unclear. Anthropologists call them "Coosans." But "Coos" probably comes from the word for a bay used by their pushy Athapascan-speaking neighbors to the south. In any case, fur traders had visited their territory since at least 1826. Jedediah Smith and his associates passed through in 1828 on their way to a confrontation with some not-so-friendly Indians in what became known as the Umpqua massacre. Then there were the professional Indian fighters cast ashore on the North Spit in early 1852, warriors from another world with lots of guns and big fierce dogs. We may imagine the Coosans' relief when the soldiers' chief appeared and led these warriors away on the rugged trail that went south.

Thus, the "Coosans" may have come to think of whites as natives of some distant, unknown place, passing through their territory en route to unknown destinations. In contrast, the Coosans were people who, except for a seasonal migration inland to dig for camas bulbs, stayed where they were. Why should they go anywhere else? Nature treated them as she did other creatures of this rich littoral, providing an abundance of good things to eat, which varied according to the season. The vast forest around them on three sides was enchanted, but they used what they needed of it for their wooden houses, canoes, clothes, weapons, and implements. On the basis of linguistic evidence, it appears that they had lived at Coos Bay for thousands of years.[11] In their creation myths, human life seems to have *begun* at Coos Bay.[12]

Now more moving people had arrived. They looked at everything, and then they asked the Coosan chiefs to make their marks on documents. Maybe they would give the Coosans some of their powerful drink ...

CONTRARY TO WHAT may have been the expectation of the Coosans, the "moving people" who appeared at South Slough in 1853 were not just passing through. Not that the whites wanted to shackle the Coosans and work them to death, as the Spaniards had done to large sections of the native population of Latin America, or to trick them into virtual slavery, as the British would do to the natives of Rhodesia.

Western Oregon crawled with non-native fortune seekers who would soon be eager for a job, any kind of job, in a mine or mill. All the pioneer developers of the Coos Bay Commercial Company wanted of the natives was their homeland. That was all.

They had quickly seized on its potential. As Harris would recall, "[t]he bay presented them a grand and promising appearance. They ... also noticed the massive forests of cedar and fir on every hand, the marvelous schools of fish, and extensive clam flats."[13] I've already mentioned their discovery of surface veins of coal.

Harris selected as a future townsite a half section (that is, half a square mile) of the place where "romantic" Coosan villages lined the bay. He then journeyed 200 miles north to the nearest land office, where he filed a claim under the 1850 Donation Act, which granted extensive acreage to every white settler or occupant of public lands, "half breeds included."[14] His site had the best natural anchorage on the Bay. The only question was what to call the place. He and his associates lay on the beach one day, brainstorming a name for the town they were about to build. They hit on something good—Empire City. Empire City would serve as county seat until 1896. Other members of the company claimed sites that would become Marshfield, North Bend, and farming acreage on the Coos River. All of them "purchased their claims of the Indians" through informal agreements which were "kept inviolate on the part of the Indians."[15]

The delicacy of Harris's wording speaks volumes for the fate of the agreements under which Coos Bay's natives gave up their native lands. What could they have received in return? We must imagine that they got what native people usually did in such circumstances—whiskey, clothes, and wampum. Like nineteenth-century Congo chiefs, like tribal chieftains everywhere, the Coosan leaders "understood neither the language nor the concept of giving their land to someone else..."[16]

The arrival of the Jacksonville developers was a decisive event. Soon "'[a]ll the world and the rest of mankind' [were] going off to Cowse Bay,"[17] and the area was well on its way to being ethnically cleansed. The white takeover of the Coosans' native land reflected a seldom-stated principle, though one well known to H. H. Luse and every corporation, landlord, and colonist. It goes like this: He who gains legal title to the land, by whatever means, has a right to evict anyone who may be living there and to extract for profit whatever resources the land contains. Some would even go so far as to maintain that the colonized had no right to their land because they had no concept of property rights![18] Of course, as Luse found out, one could not so easily evict white businessmen with the means to dispute the legality of an opposing claim.

But as Aimé Césaire declared in 1955, "no one colonizes with impunity."[19] The principle established at Coos Bay and throughout much of the world by European colonizers would, in time, facilitate the corporate plundering of Coos Bay's natural wealth.

ENDNOTES

1. A.G. Walling, *History of Southern Oregon* (Portland: Walling, 1884) 360

2. Walling 491

3. Walling 491

4. Quoted in Dodge 129.

5. Quoted in Dodge 130.

6. Quoted in Dodge 131.

7. Quoted in Dodge 131.

8. Quoted in Dodge 120.

9. Quoted in Rodney 79. On the other hand, members of a Columbia River tribe surprised William Clark by refusing red beads. They would trade for only blue or white. See John Bakeless, ed., *The Journals of Lewis and Clark: A new selection with an introduction by John Bakeless* (New York: Mentor, 1964) 284. Compare the restriction of yellow clothing to the emperor and empress of Ch'ing dynasty China.

10. Quoted in Beckham, *Coos Bay* 9

11. See Lawrence C. Thompson and M. Dale Kinkade, "Languages," in *Handbook of the North American Indians*, vol. 7, ed. William C. Sturtevant (Washington: Smithsonian, 1990) 45. In addition, evidence of campsites dating back 3,000 years has been found at Reedsport, just twenty miles to the north. See Portland *Oregonian*, August 1,1979: C22.

12. See Beckham, *The Indians of Western Oregon: This Land Was Theirs* (Coos Bay: Arago Books, 1977) 4-5; Leo J. Frachtenberg, *Coos Texts, Vol. 1* (New York: Columbia University Press, 1913) 8, 49 ff.

13. Quoted in Dodge 131.

14. See Hubert H. Bancroft, *History of Oregon*, Vol. II, 1848–1888 (San Francisco: The History Co., 1888) 260 ff.

15. Quoted in Dodge 132-33.

16. Victoria Brittain, "Colonialism and the Predatory State in the Congo," rev. of *King Leopold's Ghost*, by Adam Hochschild, *New Left Review* 236 (July/August 1999): 138.

17. From a letter of Matthew P. Deady, the same U.S. district judge who, accusing Perry Marple of an incapacity to distinguish right from wrong, had him disbarred. Quoted in Beckham, *Coos Bay* 14.

18. Tabb 95.

19. Aimé Césaire, *Discourse on Colonialism*, Joan Pinkham, trans. (New York: Monthly Review Press, 2000) 39.

CHAPTER 7

The Metal Tooth Creases the Earth

I N **1856** some Tututsi Indians killed several whites at Gold Beach, at the mouth of the Rogue River, about eighty miles down the coast from Coos Bay. The 130 survivors of this uprising huddled in a fort to await reinforcements. They stayed there long enough for two weddings to take place, in each case between a white man and an Indian woman. Coos Bay residents were more impressed with the danger to whites than with the romantic possibilities of extended contact. They "expected that the Coos and Coquille tribes would at any moment ... commence their butchery" on them![1] So persuaded were they of this threat that they took to locking up the women and children in a fort at Empire City every night. They also organized a civil patrol. The Coosan villagers responded by assembling in a nearby camp, to await the kind of treaty other tribal people had received. Instead, they got tuberculosis and eviction.

My reading of this history is that the Coosans did what they had to do to avoid being massacred themselves. If there was one thing they had learned about the whites it was beware their fear. Angry they were dangerous, but when whites were afraid, look out. The Coosans had surrendered to pre-empt something worse.

Soldiers marched surviving Coos Bay natives to Fort Umpqua, some twenty miles to the north. Within a few years they marched them another fifty miles up the coast to Yachats Prairie. There they were merged with members of other tribes and ordered to plant crops. White settlers drove survivors out of Yachats Prairie in 1875. Some drifted back to Coos Bay.

I imagine one such survivor who never left Coos Bay because, when the rest of her people were evicted, she was living with a white man. Such unions were not limited to besieged forts. In fact, in 1864, when members of a U. S. Army unit came to seize their "squaws" and march them to the reservation up the coast, local "lumbermen" (loggers, probably) resisted with threats and tears.[2]

Annie I will call this character, after Annie Miner Peterson, whose retelling of Coosan legends and stories for anthropologist Melville Jacobs in the 1930s provides a substantial part of what little there is to read about the Coosan people and their culture. Annie's mother was one of those who stayed behind.

> *By the time the others were sent off to the reservation in the north, she was already used to the sight of people pacing off distances and driving an occasional stake into the ground, as they divided the earth into the countless fragments they called "plots." Annie had also learned the names of the new kinds of animals that the white man brought with him. But the bearers of those names—pigs, cows, goats, sheep, chickens, and horses—trampled favorite native root grounds. They devoured shoots that she and her sisters had used to collect. They spoiled the streams for fish. And their excrement was everywhere. Annie didn't like the white man's animals.*
>
> *But their tools were made of a marvelous hard stone that allowed white men to make the largest tree come crashing down. At the gold camps to the south, two men using what they called a "whipsaw" could shape a board in less time than her people used to take to begin such a task. In the Coquille River valley, they used the miracle stone pulled by a horse or mule to put mysterious furrows in the earth.*
>
> *The Coosans had always grown tobacco, but not by clearing fields first. And look what the moving people cleared: roots, shoots, berries, seeds, nuts: everything given by the earth to eat, besides destroying the homes of animal cousins and uncles and aunts. Why work so hard for food when it was right there under their noses? A Coosan hated laziness as much as anyone, but the whites wore out their days unnecessarily.*
>
> *The newspaper, which her husband read to her, said it better than she could. Whites were engaged in a "feverish struggle for self-advancement." Their greed was a kind of pox that made her husband think of dashing halfway round the world at any whispering of gold in distant parts. To get rich was good: she accepted that. She remembered Coosans who had lived to find a "wealth-charm." But even if they did,*

any chance of climbing up the social tree was pretty much limited to marrying into wealth. Which in itself could be disastrous. For a poor-born maiden, marriage to a rich man could mean enslavement to his higher-ranking wives. Newly gotten wealth could get a person killed. "Rich-person's child" was a poisonous curse.[4] Wealth was good, but only a lonely man would spend his days in search of it.

Anyone can get ahead; that's what the moving people said. Anyone can go from poverty to wealth. But clearly everyone could not get ahead of everybody else without some people being trampled under foot. Only a few got rich, just as it had always been. And the only way that she could hope to get rich was by marrying a rich white man. But rich white men didn't marry Indians. Only poor men did.[5]

Annie remembered how she and the other females had spent their days—gathering shellfish, berries, firewood and roots, and preparing the food. All this while the men were hunting and fishing, building houses and canoes, and battling with their enemies. Between a husband and a wife, there was nothing left undone.

White women also did the cooking. They made and mended clothes and washed them too. But white women worked alone unless they had some daughters or their husband could afford a maid. White women had no other wives to boss or fear.

As for white men, there were two basic types. There were those who traded their time to others, and there were the others who could hire them. The first, called workers, were something like slaves, except that they had not been captured in war and could come and go as they pleased. But wherever they went, if they found work it was the work of slaves—dirty, dangerous work that no one else would do. Thus, they spent their waking hours cutting down the giant trees or working in a lumber mill or poking with a pick the innards of the mother earth. Then they would come home grimy and exhausted by their day. For this they received money, but not the kind of money Annie's people used to use. You could not pay off an injury to someone else with a string of shells anymore. Now even a white deer hide could only be traded for a metal coin or two.

But those who had the white man's coins could buy most anything. They could go to Luse's General Merchandise in Empire City, E.B. Dean and Company's Marshfield Mill Store, or take a boat around the bend to the Simpson store (though not even a white man could buy whiskey there). The stores had nearly everything: groceries, boots and shoes, all kinds of clothes, furniture, bedding, tools, wallpaper, lamps, and "fancy goods." You name it. Most all of it came in on sailing ships from far away, but some of the ships didn't make it out to sea again. They wrecked, and people got free lumber to improve their shacks.

Not that the white man's money could only be used to buy goods in a store. Enough of it and you could buy just anything—the tallest tree, the work of men, a fragment of the earth herself, even an advantageous law. As someone said, "Ought one not to have command of the world when his pockets were full?"⁵ Far from commanding anyone but her, the men that Annie knew would tend to pour their earnings into alcohol and other women's bodies.

As for the other kind of man, the boss, his hands stayed clean. He could go around in nice clothes. He held the keys to both the mill and its store. Working men said that whatever money they earned jumped from one of the owner's pockets right into the other when they bought the things they needed at the owner's store.

Annie was alarmed by how the white man treated the earth and its inhabitants. He regarded the forest as so many acres of timber. Timber was what got turned to logs and sold to a mill operator, whose saws would make them into boards, posts and shingles, each one the spit and image of the rest, which were then shipped off to someone far away. The mills of Simpson, Luse, and E.B. Dean were filling ships with lumber every week, and everybody said that this was just the start. The start of what? The pitch-dress ogresses of Coosan forest lore had surely long since fled.

As for the waterways, which were the source of most of what her people used to eat, tree cutters dumped so many logs in them that even a small boat could not get through at times. Wood sediment was filling up the bay itself.

Of course, the trees the whites cut down and the coal they dug out of the ground provided lots of jobs for working men. But just when things were going fine, the mill or mine closed down. Then, as someone said, the workers had to live "on clams and faith."⁷ How different things had been when Annie was a girl. "Where there is a house emitting smoke, there one can go and eat"—or so the saying went. Which was true, and they could take a food gift home besides. A house? Of course each family had a house, a cozy house of lashed-together boards set in the dug out earth. Now Captain Harris was telling anybody who *would listen that his crude log cabin was "the first house built in Coos County."[8]*

For the whites, there were themselves and there was "nature," which was almost everything they weren't. When they shot a deer, caught a fish, downed a tree, or pried some minerals from the flanks of mother earth, they didn't even thank the deer or salmon or the earth. They seemed to think these things existed just for them, like the goods in their stores.[9] And when they got together in their wooden meeting house, it was only to the sky god that they said their thanks. The white man's earth was just a treasure chest. Since Annie's people hadn't opened it, they had lost their right to live where they had always been.[10]

What might our Annie have said if she had learned to read and stumbled on an English publication of the previous century, which contained the argument that nature could be "too prodigal with her gifts"?[11] *If nature were "too prodigal," the author seemed to say, there would be no chance for men to get rich off of her. Everything that was needed could be had for free, and so it could not be sold. Which was how she thought it had been at Coos Bay before the white man came to stake his claims and clear his plots and loose his animals on the land. But such was not the case, apparently. The earth had not been prodigal enough to keep the white man out.*

Annie might have seen and thought all this, but our Annie is only an invention. Coos Bay's pioneer history includes mention of a real Coosan female, though, a woman who did not live long enough to become an observer of the white economy or participant in reservation life either one. It was her misfortune to be present one fine dawn in early 1854 when some gold miners at Whiskey Run (a few miles down the coast from Coos Bay) invaded the camp she occupied with fifteen Coosan men and fatally shot them all. Standing behind any principles of right and wrong in the transformation of the Coosan homeland into other people's property was force: Whites had the guns.[12]

Freed of its native inhabitants, Coos Bay became a land of possibilities. For some there was a chance to find work in a mill or logging camp. Others would plough and plant the fertile bottom lands. For a few, there was the kind of investment opportunity described in Chapter 3. A time would come again when people at Coos Bay, some people anyway, would think of nature as a web or continuum which included themselves, but with the coming of white settlement, that time was a long way off.

But wait, is this fair? The Coosans took their share of skins, roots, seeds, fish, wood, etc. To judge by accounts of the earliest contacts, they may have taken even more than their share. They had plenty of food and skins to trade for white man's things, at least. Fishers and gatherers take what the earth and waterways provide. Where the Coosans differed from the whites, economically, was not so much a matter of technology as of living within the limits of natural provisions. The Coosans had a steady-state economy: it didn't have to grow or die. Both their production and consumption were sustainable. For a peek at what such a society might look like today, see Ernest Callenbach's *Ecotopia*.[13]

Under a regime—call it capitalism, call it the market system, call it what you will—in which natural goods lose their sacredness or mere usefulness to become commodities, a place that has such goods will likely see them taken for gain by people more powerful than anyone locally. With the arrival of the Jacksonville developers, Coos Bay's natural goods became subject to private ownership and sale, or processing and sale for even more. The area was ripe for plundering.

ENDNOTES

1. Quoted in Dodge 136.

2. Royal A. Bensell, *All Quiet on the Yamhill: The Journal of Corporal Royal A. Bensell,* ed. Gunther Barth (Eugene: University of Oregon Books, 1959) 146-47.

3. Seen by the *Coos Bay News* (30 June 1875) as responsible for the "national want of cheerfulness."

4. Melville Jacobs, "Coos Narrative and Ethnologic Texts," *University of Washington Publications in Anthropology* 8.1 (April 1939) 84-86, 111; cf. 61-62. Compare Occitania (now southern France) of six hundred years ago, where "[c]ondemnation of ostentatious wealth and the power which accompanied it seems to have been general." From Emmanuel LeRoy Ladurie, *Montaillou: The Promised Land of Error,* trans. Barbara Bray (New York: Vintage Books, 1979) 332. Such attitudes were formerly widespread.

5. The real Annie—the "beautiful and accomplished" Annie Miner Peterson—may have married seven times. See Roberta L. Hall, *The Coquille Indians: Yesterday, Today and Tomorrow* (Corvallis, Ore: Words and Pictures, 1991) 83-84.

6. The quote is from Ramón J. Sender, *Seven Red Sundays,* trans. Peter C. Mitchell (Hammondsworth, Eng.: Penguin, 1938) 131.

7. Beckham, *Coos Bay* 43.

8. Quoted in Dodge 133.

9. "Our markets, our shopping avenues and malls mimic a new-found nature of prodigious fecundity." From Jean Baudrillard, *Selected Writings*, 2nd edn., ed. Mark Poster, trans. Jacques Mourrain (Stanford, Calif.: Stanford University Press, 2001) 33.

10. Cf. the statement of a one-time administrator of French Indochina that the right of the colonized to possess the land on which they lived "would leave unutilized resources to lie forever idle in the hands of incompetents." Quoted in Césaire 39.

11. Nathaniel Forster, *An Enquiry into the Causes of the Present High Price of Provisions*, cited in Karl Marx, *Capital: A Critique of Political Economy*, Vol. One (New York: Vintage, 1977) 649.

12. They had the guns that worked anyway. Members of the Coos Bay Commercial Company found that Coosans they encountered had a half dozen old English guns. [12] See Dodge 129. Europeans often gave such "trading guns" to tribal people in the seventeenth and eighteenth centuries.

13. William Weston, *Ecotopia: The Notebooks and Reports of William Weston* (New York: Bantam, 1990).

Approaching North Bend from the north

Courtesy of Dick Kimker

The house with the gambrel roof

Author's photo

Closed for March—North Bend storefront

Author's photo

Plenty of parking in downtown North Bend
Author's photo

Empty store, downtown Coos Bay
Author's photo

Where the fishing fleet used to dock
Author's photo

Another empty store, downtown Coos Bay   *Author's photo*

"Painted over many times"   *Author's photo*

Under McCullough Bridge   *Author's photo*

Toward the Little Island
Author's photo

Female workers at Evans Products plant, c. 1944
Coos Historical Museum

North Bend docks, World War II

Coos Historical Museum

Weyco's Coos River log shipping site

Courtesy of Shirley Richards

Piloting a big one

Courtesy of Shirley Richard

Aerial view of North Bend, c. 1950

Coos Historical Museu

Fishing boats on the bay, c. 1955

Courtesy of Dick Kimker

Captain A.M. Simpson
Coos Historical Museum

The Western Shore, painting by W.S. Stephens
Coos Historical Museum

Bill Vaughan logging crew with steam donkey

Courtesy of Gordon Ros

72

Logging locomotive pushing logs

Courtesy of Mike Vaughan

Millington Mill being built

Courtesy of Gordon Ross

C.A. Smith's Big Mill

Coos Historical Museum

C.A. Smith Co. mill office

Courtesy of Gordon Ross

Eastport coal bunker

Courtesy of Gordon Ross

San Francisco's Montgomery St., 1856

Golden Gate from Telegraph Hill, 1867

wo views of San Francisco Bay, about sixty years apart

San Franciso History Center, San Francisco Public Library

Looking south from Marshfield's Telegraph Hill, 1914

Courtesy of Gordon Ross

Downtown
Marshfield looking
north, 1955

*Courtesy of Dick
Kimker and permission
of Coos Historical
Museum*

Downtown
Marshfield looking
north, 1936

*Courtesy of Dick Kimker
and permission of Coos
Historical Museum*

Stage line along the Umpqua River

Courtesy of Mike Vaughar

Goldie Riggs, queen of Coos Bay's ra
linkage *Courtesy of Gordon Ro*

Louie Simpson drives a spike, marking long awaited
rail link *Courtesy of Gordon Ross*

First train to come to North Bend

The *Santa Clara*

Wreck of the *Santa Clara*

Towing rock for the bar's north jetty, c. 1925

Courtesy of Gordon Ross

Arrival of new cars in North Bend, 1912

Courtesy of Mike Vaugha

Railroad trestle

Courtesy of Mike Vaughan

The real Annie: Annie Miner
Peterson *Coos Historical Museum*

Hunting camp: Frank Black and Wes Riggs, c. 1900
Courtesy of Gordon Ross

Oxen pulling logs

Coos Historical Museum

oisting a log

Courtesy of Mike Vaughan

nidentified miners

Coos Historical Museum

"Old Blind Kate"

Coos Historical Museum

The *Czarina*

Courtesy of Gordon Ros

Coos Bay civic leaders in Odd Fellows garb, 1889

Courtesy of Gordon Ros

Fong Sing, mill cook, c. 1900
Courtesy of Mike Vaughan

County Historical Society picnic on north jetty, 1892
Courtesy of Gordon Ross

Logging crew on stump   *Courtesy of Mike Vaughan*

Rafting logs with the tide

Courtesy of Gordon Ros

Picnic at Charleston Bay

Courtesy of Gordon Ros

Coos Bay's shipbuilding crews, 1918

Dale Richards, scaler and log rafter, 1962
Courtesy of Shirley Richards

On the picket line with Marilyn and Leslie Richards   *Courtesy of Shirley Richards*

Frederick Weyerhaeuser,
1834 -1914
The Newcomen Society, 1981

Douglas fir and tree fallers in the Pacific Northwest,
early 1900s   *The Newcomen Society, 1981*

Log dump   *Courtesy of Mike Vaughan*

Making plywood out of Southern pine

The Newcomen Society, 1981

Logs stacked by the bay

Author's photo

Loading logs: Tony Richards in profile   *Courtesy of Shirley Richards*

A load of logs crosses the bar   *Courtesy of Shirley Richards*

Sowing future trees by helicopter in the 1950s

The Newcomen Society, 1981

One of Weyerhaeuser's seedling nurseries

The Newcomen Society, 1981

G-P collects mahogany logs in the Philippines, c. 1965

The Newcomen Society, 1981

Range of Port Orford cedar,
c. 1922

The Timberman, April, 1922

A G-P tree improvement center

The Newcomen Society, 1981

Coos Bay's chip pile, ready for export

Courtesy of Shirley Richards

Coos Bay loading dock

From saws to slots

Towing the last log raft from Weyco's Allegany site   *Courtesy of Shirley Richar*

CHAPTER 8

The Class War at Coos Bay

I N CHAPTER 5 I discussed a shipwreck that, for a few days, democratized plundering at Coos Bay. Now I want to talk about another tragic wreck. The steam collier *Czarina* was bound for San Francisco with her usual cargo of lumber and coal when she approached the bar one windy January day in 1910. She also carried twenty-three crewmen and one passenger. But this lone passenger was the son of C.J. Millis, general manager of Southern Pacific Railroad Company's operations in the area, which included ownership of the *Czarina*. When her captain informed him that the breakers sweeping over the bar were too high to permit safe passage of the ship, Millis ordered him to take the ship out anyway. He didn't want his son to miss any classes at the University of California in Berkeley, you see.

The captain did as he was told. Consequently, witnesses on shore could only watch in horror as the *Czarina* lost course, struck the channel's south spit (just as the *Santa Clara* would), and then, in a desperate attempt to save the cargo, dropped anchor. This was a mistake: now the ship was too close to shore to allow the possibility of rescue by another ship and too far out in the heavy surf to permit rescue by land. Nor could crew members hoist up the anchor. In fact, the high waves forced them to take refuge in the rigging, where the ocean's overpowering pulse hurled lumber at them from the deck, driving them one by one out of the rigging and into the sea. All but one man drowned, and the U. S. Life Saving Service called it the most "appalling marine casualty" in twenty-five years.[1]

The *Czarina* tragedy serves as an extreme example of the disparity of power at Coos Bay. As the local representative of the kind of remotely controlled company that determined the area's economic destiny, C.J. Millis was a member of a small but important elite. G.W. Loggie of SOIC was another, as was Al Powers of the C.A. Smith Lumber Company. Jobseekers crowded Marshfield's post office every day at 7 a.m. in the hope of catching Mr. Powers before he could embark for one of Smith's logging camps. Not to forget J.W. Forester of the Coos Bay Lumber Company. In his day he was "the ultimate man to see."[2] Such men called the shots at Coos Bay, often with local casualties. Except for Millis' son, their offspring were not among the casualties.

To find contemporary representatives of this caste, you might look to the board of directors of Coos Bay's South Coast Development Council. Voting members pay $10,000 for the privileges—or is it the opportunities?—afforded by such an investment. Asked where the local economy was headed, a local business owner said that only such insiders know.

Millis, Forester, et al., occupied middle rungs of a hierarchy that had, at its heights, the likes of C.A. Smith; Henry Huntington, the Southern Pacific heir; and later, George H. Weyerhaeuser, the company founder's great grandson; and Robert Flowerree, chair and CEO of Georgia-Pacific from 1976 to 1983. Below the corporations' men was Coos Bay's own social hierarchy. In the early years members of the local gentry tended to come from New England. They had their businesses, professional practices, and their men's and women's clubs. Summer weekends brought them out for picnic excursions on the bay, where everybody waved and smiled for the camera, just as people do today. They escaped to San Francisco whenever they could.

Coos Bay's workers, on the other hand, were men on the move, at least at first. "Thousands of workers came to the region and then left with hardly a trace of having been there," says local historian Douthit.[3] In fact, they left plenty of traces when they had the chance—evidence of their work on all the lumber, coal, and other products shipped to California and elsewhere in growing quantities.

The reader of the area's late nineteenth-century news source can easily distinguish representatives of these classes. Unless involved in some small scandal, members of the gentry always have names. They have opinions. They make social contributions and attend public events. Members of the working class participate anonymously in non-fatal shootings, stabbings, and the occasional free-for-all. They acquire names when the shooting, stabbing, etc., results in a death or when one of them is killed or maimed at work. There are either too many of them for available jobs or too few. As the historian Cox dryly remarked, "[t]he gulf between common laborers and the upper levels of society was undoubtedly great."[4]

Because Coos Bay's labor force consisted mostly of single men, a thriving service industry of taverns and prostitutes found fertile ground to flourish there. Working girls plied their trade in brothels, dance halls, streets, windows, hotels, tents, and "float houses." North Bend had a reputation "as a wide open coastal frontier town."[5] This gave the local gentry a ready target for denunciation and talk of reform.

By the 1940s North Bend's red light district probably consisted of a single location, known by reputation even to pre-pubescent boys. Not that the reform efforts had enjoyed success. Most workers at Coos Bay had families by then. But there were still a lot of taverns and plenty of evidence of alcohol abuse. I remember sitting in the family car outside a store one afternoon and noticing a man with a silly grin who was having a problem getting across the street. For some reason he kept falling down. "What's the matter with that man?" I asked. "That man is drunk, don't look at him," my mom advised.

From the beginning, Coos Bay's workers were divided by race. In 1900 a mob ran African-American miners out of the area. (Employers had lured them to Coos Bay from afar with lavish, unmet promises.) The *Coos Bay News* all but advocated anti-Chinese incidents, such as the anonymous arson threats received by Marshfield businesses that employed Chinese in 1877; the expulsion of Chinese by miners at Johnson's Creek, just south of the lower Coquille, in 1879; the boys who assaulted Chinese pedestrians with "rocks, clubs, etc."[6] (The *News* admonished them to stop, lest they bring trouble on themselves.) Northern European immigrants, on the other hand, were embrace by the *News*'s open arms. Most welcome of all at Coos Bay were "men with capital to develop its resources."[7] The fact that the workforce included members of an especially vulnerable, thus more exploitable race, must have made Coos Bay somewhat more attractive to such men with capital.

As for Coos Bay's upscale class, they were not divided by race because they were of only one race. They acquired their income from the sale of goods, professional services, and the collection of rents. They were a self-renewing class with local roots.

Social and economic inequality got played out, as it always does, in countless, mostly invisible but sometimes spectacular ways. How spectacular? Be a spectator at some events of the summer of 1913, when, following a venomous editorial campaign by the *Coos Bay Times* against the Industrial Workers of the World (IWW) for its agitation on behalf of local workers for an eight-hour day and higher pay, Marshfield police jailed two IWW organizers. Many local businessmen had already been appointed "special law enforcement officers."[8] Now a crowd of them abducted the pair from their jail cells to put them on a boat and take them to a remote spot where they ordered them to leave the county, as they were, on foot. But not before they kissed the flag.

When Bailey K. Leach, a chiropractor and Socialist newspaper editor, expressed criticism of this outrageous violation of all requirements of due process and other basic rights, business leaders took him from his Bandon home, brought him to Marshfield, and deported him just as they had the other two. Leach accused C.A. Smith Lumber's Al Powers, Bandon lumber magnate George W. Moore, and other county luminaries of being behind this further instance of vigilante justice. The *Times* questioned his "right to sneer at things that decent, self-respecting citizens hold sacred and which make for law and order."[9] Michael Parenti explains this better than I can: "[c]hallenges to the privileged social order are treated as attacks on all social order, a plunge into chaos and anarchy."[10] Still, Coos Bay's treatment of the IWW representatives and their supporters was no more than a tap on the wrist compared to what sometimes happened to Wobbly organizers elsewhere.[11]

What did local workers think of these events? Employees of Moore's Bandon lumber company stood solidly by "to back up the businessman"[12] as he, collectively, deported Leach. Appointed to investigate the matter, the state's attorney general reported that every one of the many loggers and mill workers with whom he had spoken "claimed to be working under the best conditions." His report concluded that "[t]he loggers and millmen are a contented class in Coos County, and apparently dislike the invasion of agitators and disturbers."[13]

Well might we wonder how the IWW could gain even the slightest toehold in such a hostile environment. Could the attorney general have missed something? And how. By 1918 the IWW was back. The C.A. Smith Company defused an organizing drive at its premier logging site by meeting some of its demands. Henceforth, loggers would get a weekly change of sheets, a warmed and deloused bunkhouse, and china plates. The company further demonstrated its good will by rushing one injured worker to the hospital.

Coos Bay's isolation and climate made for seasonal labor shortages, and sometimes workers won their demands. The Coos Bay waterfront was another matter altogether. There workers' grievances piled up until 1934, when Pacific coast longshore workers went out on strike. Firing up striking Coos Bay longshoremen were events 500 miles to the south, where workers battled furiously with the San Francisco police and National Guard. Their general strike deserves remembering. At Coos Bay, lumber piled up on the docks. Employers brought in strike breakers, of course: rocks flew, and in Empire unionists overturned a bus. Invigorated by awareness that they could shut down the local economy, workers formed several locals of the Congress of Industrial Organizations (CIO). Four decades removed, G-P's corporate biographer thought that the presence of longshoremen had made Coos Bay's unions "especially militant."[14]

After World War II, employers and their publicists, often backed by governmental agencies, were able to play off the more conservative American Federation of Labor (AFL) locals against those of the CIO. Events at Coos Bay came to a head in 1948 with the "*Rolando* incident," in which CIO maritime unionists and members of the International Longshoremen's and Warehousemen's Union (ILWU) picketed the below-deck work of an AFL crew, surrounding the Irwin-Lyons mill and dock to prevent loading of the ship. The head of the AFL sailors' union charged that "CIO communist stooges on the waterfront" had instigated the dispute.[15] Another AFL official pulled out all the stops, claiming that the CIO's "communist element" was "importing negroes to picket in Coos Bay," so as to cause a race riot.[16]

With disputed reports of violence, state troops were brought in. The coast-length strike, of which this was a skirmish, threw 1,500 out of work at Coos Bay. But the strike or potential strike was about the only effective weapon in the workers' hands. A day would come when employers would have no more use for their hands. With factory closures, the mill workers' strike would become as outmoded as trench warfare and the typewriter.

By the time I came on the scene, Coos Bay's workers were no longer divided by race. The friendly Chinese grocer seemed to be the only local representative of his kind—and of people of color, generally. I didn't think of Coos Bay as ethnically deprived, of course. Neither did it occur to me to ask my Uncle Bob about his experiences as a longshoreman, a fact I now regret. And as much as I knew about the struggles that took place on the football field and in the gym, I knew nothing of the struggles then raging on Coos Bay's docks. Neither in my classroom nor in my home do I remember any mention of these events. But bordering the *Coos Bay Times*'s accounts of the *Rolando* incident are outcroppings of more familiar terrain, including the front-page story of a fire that left a classmate's family homeless and the listings of all-but-forgotten radio shows.

There was an after-school incident one day that does seem relevant, now that I think of it. On the grassy slope behind old Central School, surrounded by a cheering schoolboy crowd, crouched three pairs of boys, squared off for separate fights. On the one side, trying to look tough, were boys whose fathers' businesses or professions were known to almost every North Bend resident. As to the fathers of the other three, they might have worked in the mills, if they were living in the area, and *if* they were, they certainly didn't live in Simpson Heights.

Nobody except the onlookers was saying anything. Class seemed to be the only issue here. Of course, I lacked such concepts at the time. The crowd seemed to favor the "proletarian" boys, but I kept my mouth shut. I knew I had more in common with the "bourgeois" boys than with the proles. Besides, the former included a distant cousin. This made it a little scary when, one by one, each of my class representatives sustained a blow and went tearfully off, muttering weak threats.

The anti-Communist rhetoric that filled the airwaves and newspaper columns of that era only mystified me. Why would anybody want to be a Communist when everybody knew that Communism was bad? I couldn't understand what Gabriel Heater got so worked up about. Then, one afternoon in the junior high school band room, when I used a transparent excuse to avoid participation in a parade, the hotheaded band teacher called *me* a Communist. And I was only a third clarinet! Even if (as some would argue now) he more or less had me pegged, the charge came on the basis of such scrawny evidence! Many years would pass before I heard and understood the old refrain that puts a different spin on redbaiting: "You ain't been doin' nothin' if you ain't been called a red."

ENDNOTES

1. Quoted in Douthit 30; cf. 28 ff.

2. Quoted in Robbins, *Hard Times* 119. Reprinted by permission of the University of Washington Press.

3. Douthit 108-9.

4. Cox, *Mills and Markets* 169. Reprinted by permission of the University of Washington Press.

5. Dick Wagner, *Louie Simpson's North Bend* (North Bend: NB News, 1986) 22; cf. Douthit 113-14.

6. *Coos Bay News*, April 6, 1892; cf. August 15, 1877, June 4, 1879.

7. *Coos Bay News*, August 12, 1885.

8. Robbins, *Hard Times* 141. Reprinted by permission of the University of Washington Press.

9. Quoted in Douthit 121.

10. In Michael Parenti, *Blackshirts & Reds: Rational Rascism and the Overthrow of Communism* (San Francisco: City Lights, 1997) 153.

11. Cf. Henry E. McGuckin, *Memoirs of a Wobbly* (Chicago: Chas. H. Kerr, 1987).

12. Quoted in Douthit 121.

13. Quoted in Douthit 121.

14. Ross 120.

15. *Coos Bay Times*, August 28, 1948: 1.

16. *Coos Bay Times*, August 30, 1948: 3.

CHAPTER 9

Growth Spurts

A T THE END OF CHAPTER 2, we were in the 1950s, and Weyerhaeuser Timber Company (Weyco) and Georgia-Pacific Corporation (G-P) were setting up major manufacturing operations at Coos Bay. The former's corporate empire consisted of enormous timber holdings; several large lumber, plywood, pulp, and container board plants scattered throughout the Pacific Northwest; and sales representatives on every continent except Antarctica. Weyco had expanded and diversified to meet changing business conditions for over half a century. Its earliest rivals had long since disappeared. G-P had made up for a much later start by "[a]cquiring company after company and forest tracts throughout the country ... ," diversifying into almost everything that could be made from trees to become one of a new breed of big "multipurpose" corporations.[1]

Weyco and G-P were big—not reassuringly big like an oak with a swing on a lower branch, nor unacceptably big like a horse moving into the house, for the size of a company like Weyco or G-P will not be obvious to a local observer. But when they became the two biggest employers of the Coos Bay area, each was already sufficiently large and dynamic that it would not have occurred to G-P executives to retain the name of the Coos Bay Lumber Company, the firm their company had absorbed, any more than Weyco executives would have thought of moving their corporate headquarters to Coos Bay. Their local operations represented valuable business assets, but it was only in combination with many other such assets that they were the key to corporate growth and viability. In short, these companies were big enough that their investments in manufacturing were more important to Coos Bay than Coos Bay was to them. This did not augur well for Coos Bay.

Unlike the pioneer developers of the Coos Bay Commercial Company, Weyco and G-P executives did not have to offer the natives whiskey and trinkets or anything else for the timber they would mill. It was already theirs, a fact so far beyond dispute that the assumption of a liberal philosopher of an earlier age that "[i]t is some hardship to be born into the world and to find all nature's gifts previously engrossed,"² would have resonated silence at Coos Bay. Local residents couldn't see the forest for the jobs. As it has turned out, the thousands of jobs provided by these megacorps came with hidden but substantial costs, to be borne by future workers and their families. But before discussing what G-P and Weyco did, let's see what helped them grow so big.

WEYCO AND G-P both had humble origins. Each was founded on the ambition, hard work, and good fortune of a single man. But at a crucial point in its development, each company had a boost from an associate of the founder, someone who could offer the fledgling firm the helping hand of public support. Let's look first at Weyco's growth boost.

James J. Hill was a late-nineteenth-century railroad entrepreneur with connections to the highest financial and political circles. (Does the name J.P. Morgan ring a bell?) To provide his Northern Pacific Railway (NP) with the means to build a railroad linking Minnesota cities and those of the Pacific Northwest, Congress had given the company vast portions of the public domain—25,600 acres for each mile of railroad construction through the western territories and 12,800 acres for each mile through existing states. This made NP the biggest timber owner in the Pacific Northwest. Congress (some members of Congress, anyway) had assumed that the railroad would sell its acreage to small buyers. But NP needed to raise capital quicker than that, and NP wanted to sell its timber to people able to turn it into freight.

Hill was living in St. Paul in 1893 when who should turn up as his next-door neighbor but a man who *could* turn timber into freight. This man was surely known to Hill already, for Frederick Weyerhaeuser and his associates controlled about half the white pine forests in the region. They had bought NP timberland in Wisconsin; they had also provided Hill's other railroad, the Great Northern, with traffic from their Washington shingle mill. And like C.A. Smith and other Great Lakes lumbermen, they were running out of trees to cut. All in all, it was quite a coincidence.

Since the lumber and railroad barons were already somewhat acquainted, the shy Weyerhaeuser did not have to send his wife to borrow a cup of sugar to initiate contact with Hill. The two were soon engaged in evening fireside chats, in the course of which Hill told Weyerhaeuser "of certain financial exigencies that might require the sale of great blocks of forest."[3] The German must have loved the sound of that. Together they visited NP's holdings in Montana, Idaho, Washington, and Oregon, viewing timber which "made [Weyerhaeuser's] Lake State holdings look like pygmy forests."[4] Weyerhaeuser became NP's timber agent and a member of its board.

Then, in January 1900, Weyerhaeuser and Hill negotiated "one of the largest single land transactions in the nation's history."[5] Hill agreed to sell Weyerhaeuser's consortium 900,000 acres of NP's virgin timber for $6 an acre. The terms were $3 million down and the balance to be paid in eight semi-annual installments at 5 percent interest. The U.S. Bureau of Corporations later estimated that, considering what the Weyerhaeuser Timber Company would eventually cut, it got this timber for about ten cents per thousand board feet.[6]

"This is not for us, nor for our children," said Frederick Weyerhaeuser of the deal he had made, "but for our grandchildren."[7] When he said "our," he meant *his*, of course. He also meant that Weyco was in no hurry to turn its timber into lumber. The market already had too much of it. What Weyco wanted was more forestland. It quickly proceeded to grab up homesteaders' claims to lots adjacent to the former NP grant. A second purchase from NP of 200,000 acres in Oregon for $5 an acre may have been "the fruit of more late-evening talks with Hill beside the fireside in St. Paul."[8] How the winter evenings must have flown for that cozy pair. By 1912 Weyco had almost two million acres of timber in the Pacific Northwest. Only NP and the Southern Pacific railroad had more.

Weyco's coup transformed the region's lumber industry. Up until then vertical integration (combining, for example, manufacturing, sales, and transportation under one corporate roof, as Asa Simpson had done) had not necessarily included resource ownership. Simpson thought that taxes and interest would devour any profit from the sale of timberland, no matter how low the purchase price.[9] But Frederick Weyerhaeuser couldn't get enough of it: "Whenever I buy timber I make a profit," he exalted; "whenever I do not buy I miss an opportunity."[10] The focus of the industry now moved "from sawmills and manufacturing to land and speculation in timber."[11] Companies without much timber "were doomed to extinction."[12]

Despite the assurance of Weyco's biographers that the company "never bought timber for speculation but for sawing and selling lumber,"[13] several years went by before it got around to serious lumber manufacturing in the Pacific Northwest. Among the hundred largest U.S. firms in 1917 there were only three whose productive processes relied more on workers than on machines. Two of them were weak and unprofitable companies. The third was Weyco, which ranked twenty-first by the size of its assets.[14]

Weyco was different from other giants in another respect, as well. Despite an ancient proverb, which holds that "[t]hings wrongfully acquired never reach the heir's heir,"[15] members of the family's male line continued to control the company for so many generations that one commentator referred to Weyco's "familyism" and compared the Weyerhaeusers to the merchant banking families of thirteenth-century Italy.[16] But in acquiring raw materials far in excess of its manufacturing needs and in availing itself, eventually, of the nineteenth century's revolution in transportation to send its products to a national market, Weyco followed the typical course of industrial behemoths in extractive industries.[17] The company's landmark timber acquisitions also recall the Marxist adage that "capitalism as a social system *requires* . . .a one-time wholesale expropriation of social property. "[18] That's what separates the original capitalist from the original gangster.

G-P's "PRIMITIVE ACCUMULATION" of social property is not greatly known. Like Frederick Weyerhaeuser (who immigrated to the U.S. as a German adolescent), G-P's founder was a man of middling origins. We'll come to know him better in Chapter 10. For now, let's say that Owen Cheatham parlayed charm and enthusiasm, a commitment to good customer service, and a knack for picking and retaining strong and capable associates into a company, Georgia-Hardwood, with a string of southern lumber mills, which turned profits of $10,000 to $20,000 a year going into World War II.[19] A photograph taken around that time shows a stocky, sharp-eyed man looking ready to pounce.[20] Export-priming measures of the New Deal's Reconstruction Finance Corporation paved Cheatham's way to European customers: he returned from Europe with orders from England, the Netherlands,

Belgium, Germany, France, and Spain.[21] But it was during the war that Georgia-Hardwood's big break came.

Walter Deadrick was in charge of buying lumber for the Army Corps of Engineers. Deadrick had a buddy by the name of Eugene Howerdd, who was Cheatham's right-hand man. Result: Georgia-Hardwood (G-H) won U.S. taxpayer-funded lumber orders to the tune of around 80 million feet. Of course, this wasn't the only help that Cheatham's company received from the wartime lumber boom, nor can I say that the Deadrick-Howerdd connection was *crucial* to G-H's ability to buy up many small and independent firms on its way to becoming Georgia-Pacific after the war. But except for the sawdust, 80 million feet of lumber is nothing at which to sneeze. In fact, it's about what C.A. Smith's Big Mill could produce in 235 eight-hour shifts.

Providing public subsidies to major corporations certainly hasn't been confined to Weyco, G-P, and the intercontinental railroads. Producers of such recent "market miracles" as the Internet, computers, lasers, satellites, and transistors have received such help and on a massive scale, too.[22]

But wait a minute. If the companies hadn't done what they had to do to obtain supplies and produce wood products, where would we be? Where would *I* be? As I said earlier, my father had a lumberyard. He built wood cabinets. He built houses out of wood. I live in a house made primarily of wood. If it weren't for wood. . . But let us not confuse two things.

The products of companies like Weyco and G-P may serve human needs, but they do so only incidentally. In a market economy, manufacturers produce goods to sell: whether the buyer is a person who already owns three homes and a dozen apartment buildings, or is a first-time home buyer is irrelevant. If the purpose of manufacturing building materials were to meet human needs, there wouldn't be any people sleeping in doorways.

Also, the extent to which we use wood products, some of them from old-growth trees, is heavily influenced by a lack of available alternatives. Any house that I might buy would probably have a lot of wood in it, but when we had our worn-out redwood deck replaced, we used a lumber substitute. This put us right in step with the industry's shift from lumber manufacturing to the production of processed materials. I can only touch on this big subject here.

ENDNOTES

1. *New York Times*, October 25,1970; Cox et al, *This Well-Wooded Land: Americans and Their Forests from Colonial Times to the Present* (Lincoln, Neb.: University of Nebraska Press, 1985) 245.

2. John Stuart Mill, *Principles of Political Economy*, quoted in Russell Jacoby, *The End of Utopia: Politics and Culture in an Age of Apathy* (New York: Basic Books, 1999) 18.

3. Ralph W. Hidy, Frank E. Hill, and Allan Nevins, *Timber and Men: The Weyerhaeuser Story* (New York: MacMillan, 1963) 207.

4. Sarah J. Salo, *Timber Concentration in the Pacific Northwest: With Special Reference to the Southern Pacific Railroad, the Northern Pacific Railroad and the Weyerhaeuser Timber Co.*, published dissertation, Columbia University (Ann Arbor: Edwards Bros., 1945) 14.

5. Ellis Lucia, *Head Rig, the Story of the West Coast Lumber Industry* (Portland, Ore.: Overland, 1965) 55.

6. Lucia 55. A board foot is a unit of wood a foot square and one inch thick.

7. Quoted in Salo 14.

8. Hidy et al. 224.

9. Douthit 47.

10. Quoted in Salo 3.

11. Robert E. Ficken, "Weyerhaeuser and the Pacific Northwest Timber Industry, 1899-1903," *Experiences in a Promised Land: Essays in Pacific Northwest History*, eds. G. Thomas Edwards and Carlos A. Schwantes (Seattle: University of Washington Press, 1986) 139. Reprinted by permission of the University of Washington Press.

12. Ficken 151. Reprinted by permission of the University of Washington Press.

13. Hidy et al 144.

14. Chandler 347, 505, 569.

15. François Rabelais, *Gargantua and Pantagruel*, trans. Burton Raffel (New York: W.W. Norton, 1990)

16. Herbert Heaton, rev. of *Timber and Men*, in *Forest History* 7.3 (Fall 1963): 19.

17. Cf. Norman Girvan, *Corporate Imperialism: Conflict and Expropriation: Transnational Corporations and Economic Nationalism in the Third World* (New York: Monthly Review Press, 1976) 14-15.

18. Nancy Holmstrom and Richard Smith, "The Necessity of Gangster Capitalism: Primitive Accumulation in Russia and China," *Monthly Review* 51.9 (February 2000): 8.

19. Ross 13.

20. In *Wedge, Sr.* (Augusta, GA: Georgia-Hardwood, c. 1943) 21.

21. Ross 6.

22. Noam Chomsky, "Power in the Global Arena," *New Left Review* (July/August 1998) 14.

CHAPTER 10

Freda and the Dark Experiment

I DON'T WANT this chapter's title to mislead. Nobody conducted an experiment on Freda. Freda and the dark experiment were two separate events. Each had a role to play in the real-life story of people being dispossessed of their livelihood at places like Coos Bay. Especially at Coos Bay.

As you may recall, when G-P opened operations at Coos Bay in 1956, the company announced that it would turn its 120,000 acres of prime forestland into wood products no faster than it could grow a new generation of harvestable trees. But G-P had been guzzling smaller companies left and right, and was reeling from a cash-flow hangover. Watch how G-P's corporate biographer tiptoes around the question of what would happen next: "Whereas the original investors had been able to hold on to their assets and wait for the rise in values, G-P would have to liquidate some of the timber in order to pay for the properties and to replenish the forests."[1]

In fact, Coos Bay Lumber (the "original investors") had been a major West Coast lumber producer for almost forty years, harvesting their timber on a hundred-year cutting cycle[2] and employing thousands of the area's residents. G-P proceeded to triple what had been Coos Bay Lumber's average cut, besides selling off enough of its timber to some of Coos Bay's smaller companies to create an economic boomlet at Coos Bay. No doubt the local "properties" contributed heavily to a tenfold increase in G-P's cash flow between 1952 and 1962. And use of future timber sales to finance debt served as a model for other G-P acquisitions.

But every silver lining has a cloud attached. G-P's chainsaw approach to resolving its financial obligations got Coos Bay's civic leaders and ordinary citizens alike stirred up. And their concern caught the attention of G-P. Not just G-P but Mr. G-P, Owen Cheatham, the man who, as a lad coming up in Woodrow Wilson's time, had ignored the opinion of his grandfather that all the trees would soon be gone, to borrow, scrimp and save enough to buy an Augusta, Georgia, lumberyard for $12,000.

Young Cheatham got the lumber orders, and he was good at it, for he was a charmer, and his little Augusta lumberyard prospered. It grew to become Georgia-Hardwood Lumber Company, the direct ancestor of the company which, in 1996, became the Fortune 500's seventy-fifth largest U.S. firm. The company that Cheatham founded remains right up there with the big boys of productive capital today.

With his G-P entourage, Cheatham met with 200 members of Coos County's business and government establishment at Coquille, the county seat, in April 1957. If we had been a fly on the wall. . . . But why should we be a fly? Let's crash this party as we are and see what we can see. There's Owen Cheatham, super salesman, glad-handing one man, polishing another, and never having to light his own cigarette. While too softhearted for some of his associates, Cheatham is still the man. And if the charm doesn't work, there are other ways of taking care of G-P's business at Coos Bay and similar sources of supplies.

But listen. The G-P mogul has begun to make a speech. First of all, he announces that he doesn't "accept woeful tales that all the timber will be gone in a few years." He assures his audience that "[a] plentiful supply of second growth timber will be available by the time the first growth is gone."[3] Imagine the collective sigh of relief on hearing that—or is it disbelief? The newspaper account doesn't say.

After telling everybody what they want to hear, Cheatham lets his belt out a notch, predicting that the use of plywood, plastics, pulp, paper, and wood-based chemicals will soon make second-growth timber a greater source of wealth—for everyone, of course—than old-growth timber ever was. He looks to China's hunger for wood, also replacement of urban slums, to jack up demand for wood products. (At least he doesn't call it "urban renewal.") But there it is: nothing for Coos Bay to worry its hardhatted head about.

I remember Coquille as the sometime destination of a trip by school bus. We rocked the bus with Bulldog war cries if we were going to a

111

game. We were quieter for a band tournament. I especially remember a meeting in Coquille of two junior high school football teams. Our meeting took place in driving rain. In fact, the field was such a mud bath that Kennedy,[4] our hefty guard, caught hell from the coach at halftime because his pants were clean. Kennedy was always catching hell from the coach. By the end of the game, which the Baby Bulldogs won, my pants were muddy too, not because I got sent into the game—the score was much too close for that—but because another boy and I had gotten into a puddle-kicking fight while sitting on the bench. Then the coach sent my adversary into the game to replace Bill Rush, our halfback, who'd sprained his neck plunging into the line. The puddle kicker got a chance to get some serious football mud on him, and I had to watch him from the bench.

Coquille teams were called the Red Devils but I guess we have a sense by now of who the original "red devils" may have been.

Despite Cheatham's assurance that his company would be "glad" to pay its share of local taxes, G-P executives were back in Coos Bay in May 1961, but this time they were on the attack. G-P had petitioned the county for $5 million in tax relief. Handsome Robert Pamplin had given fair warning through an interview in Portland's *Oregonian* newspaper the month before. G-P might have to close a sawmill if the county didn't reassess their properties.[5]

At the hearing on G-P's petition, the company's attorney complained that its Bunker Hill plant (assessed by Coos County at $3 million) was fast becoming obsolete as it "was designed to handle large logs." More than half the logs it processed now were less than twelve inches wide.[6] In other words, only five years in the area and G-P was openly admitting they were running out of old-growth! Tax Commissioner J.J. Geaney, G-P's local nemesis, responded that "G-P has publicly declared it is cutting on a sustained yield basis and that if its intentions were good, it would have built a new sawmill at Bunker Hill."[7] To which the company's attorney said that G-P had every intention of remaining in Coos Bay and would upgrade its plants and buy additional timber. Of course they would.

Within a few more years, G-P's old-growth timber was almost gone. Making this sound like a pruning operation, a corporate representative explained that, as a matter of company policy, G-P had "to allow new timber to grow."[8]

Meanwhile, with Owen Cheatham's finger on the pulse of future markets, G-P was pouring capital into the manufacture of synthetic wood products. Not just plywood, which had brought the company to the Pacific Northwest in the first place (as discussed below), but in the glues and chemicals needed to manufacture plywood and G-P's other synthesized products, and to make best use of the smaller trees which, by and large, were all that G-P had left at Coos Bay and elsewhere in the region. Its Coos Bay resin plant was the first component of what would become the corporation's big chemical division, and it was as profitable as the only gas station on a desert highway. In 1966 G-P built a Coos Bay plant to export wood chips to Japan. Another local G-P plant made formaldehyde.

The shift from sawmills, with their large workforce, to the manufacture of chips, pulp, and chemicals by automated processes was not confined to Coos Bay. There was a regional tripling of capital expenditures between 1947 and 1971, but the number of manufacturing plants went down, and so did the number of jobs. Large automated operations were crowding workers out, and this had everything to do with the depletion of old-growth timber. But not to worry. In 1966, Pamplin assured a New York audience that included the next president of the U.S. that his company was "growing timber faster than we are harvesting it for our plants" on the west coast. With maturity of this "excess growth" in twenty years, G-P would add new plants.[9] Surely Mr. Pamplin wouldn't have lied to Richard Nixon, would he?

WHAT ABOUT WEYCO, the other corporate giant which, back in 1951, had opened operations at Coos Bay? As you may recall, Weyco was turning its 210,000 acres of forestland east of Coos Bay into a timber farm. In a 1961 article in *The World*, a local newspaper, Weyco's public relations department acknowledged that the spigot of jobs that the company had opened locally could "be no steadier than the flow of logs to the mills." But with sustained yield management, Weyco could prevent "serious ups and downs" to timber-dependent communities. Weyco would harvest no more than the forest could regrow and its mills process, replanting as needed to aid the regenerative powers of nature. Thus would Weyco obtain "an *uninterrupted and endless* timber supply" (emphasis added). In short, said Weyco, "[t]omorrow's jobs at the Coos Bay Branch of Weyerhaeuser Co. [would] depend on

[Weyco's] ability to manage the 210,000 acre Millicoma Tree Farm on a sustained yield basis."[10]

Basing jobs on Weyco's "ability"—was that a good idea? Short of global economic disaster, Weyco clearly had the *ability* to continue to employ Coos Bay workers for as long as Weyco wanted to. The question was not what the company *could* do but what it *would* do. An endless supply of timber meant cutting down old growth, of course. Weyco could easily outproduce nature, growing four or five trees where only a single (magnificent) one had stood. "Increasing the forest's biomass," was what they called it. Was it still a forest when planted in neat rows and cleared of undergrowth? Local millworkers couldn't care too much what it was called if it produced an endless supply of logs for Coos Bay's mills.

So, timber from here to eternity, whatever future markets might signal about the profitability of cutting down old growth before the new had reached a minimum of commercial value: it was really too good to be true.

At this point, 1961, G-P had acquired a reputation as a "fast cutter" of its timber in the Pacific Northwest, while Weyco was known as a "slow cutter,"[11] a company whose "modern executives" would "no longer 'cut out and get out.'"[12] But for reasons I'll get into in a moment, Weyco began to up its cut until it was cutting down its timber at an unsustainable rate. Just like G-P. And whether they worked for Weyco, G-P, or independently, loggers were now commuting up to four hours a day to get to the remaining old-growth stands.

By the mid-1980s, Weyco had run out of old-growth timber on its own lands. The small group of men at the top with the vantage to see such things had begun to look to public timber sales for their supplies. But this meant looking to other areas, as a far higher proportion of the Coos Bay region's timberland was privately owned than was the case elsewhere. For example, in 1985 almost twice as much of the log volume consumed by the sawmills of Coos and Curry counties (often linked as a region; linked here to avoid disclosure of private holdings) came from private industry holdings. For rival Douglas County sawmills, the proportions were reversed: more than twice the volume of *their* logs came from public forests.[13]

The question of how major producers could casually regard the public forests as a "backdrop reservoir"[14] of timber they could draw on with depletion of their own reserves has been the subject of other books.[15] The question here is, would Coos Bay's relative scarcity of publicly owned old-growth timber be a problem for Weyco, with its major operations at Springfield, Oregon? Springfield afforded easy access to Willamette National Forest, "for decades the top timber-producing forest in the country."[16] Answer: It *wouldn't* be a problem for Weyco executives that they had run out of local timber supplies if they just shut their Coos Bay operations down. It would only be a problem for Coos Bay.

However, I want to be fair. I want to give the companies the benefit of the doubt. I have to think that when Weyco and G-P opened operations at Coos Bay, they did not intend to liquidate their old-growth timber so rapidly as to leave local industry without supplies. I have to think that in making those assurances to the local communities, the companies were acting in good faith. But certain events intervened. For G-P it was a clandestine experiment. For Weyco it was a hurricane.

G-P's corporate development was tied to the manufacture and sale of a certain wood product, one that every housing builder knows. I saw my father sell it to his North Bend customers when I was young. He used it to build cabinets in his shop behind the house. My brothers and I nailed it to studs for the dollar an hour my dad paid us to help him build houses in Eureka, California, when we moved there from Coos Bay. I refer to plywood, glued together, cross-grained sheets of wood. The best plywood came from Douglas fir, the tree that named an entire region after itself.

Plywood was not invented by World War II, but it may as well have been. A wartime federal loan program encouraged builders to test new synthesized materials, cheaper than good lumber, which the contractors used to turn out prefab, pre-assembled housing for the exploding housing market. By 1948 a trade journal could gush that plywood had become "one of the most virile elements of the great forest products family," with hundreds of new uses.[17] Its production had swollen eight-fold since 1931. Plywood was the basic building matter of the new white suburbs. . .but I won't go into that.

Owen Cheatham drooled for a piece of this "insatiable market."[18] He calculated that plywood would triple the return on lumber.[19] What to do? Cheatham started buying up plywood plants in the Pacific Northwest, including two from Weyco. Soon he and his cronies on the Georgia-Hardwood board gave the company a new name: Georgia-

Pacific. They moved corporate headquarters to Portland, right in the heart of Douglas fir country. But G-P was a latecomer to the plywood manufacturing feast. Other people had their hands on nearly all the high-quality Douglas fir acreage, such as that at Coos Bay. These companies were not about to sell for any song that southern hardwood lumbermen might sing.

G-P engaged in creative financing, such as that employed in its acquisition of Coos Bay Lumber (described above), to buy what it could. The company had always done what it had to do. It even financed the manufacture of substandard plywood made from fungus-infected fir, though another company's name appeared on the panels.[20] Anything to get a leg up on the competition. But the metaphor suggests a small dog's relationship to a fire hydrant and, by the 1950s, G-P was becoming a very big dog indeed.

G-P had some cultural adjustment problems in the Pacific Northwest. The southern charm of its executives was wasted there. Even when Cheatham stationed himself beside his grand piano in the stately Georgian mansion of his Portland estate to create "a setting of sheer opulence"[21] for visiting members of the press, Oregonians weren't impressed. If only the company could find a way to make decent plywood out of something else. For example, Southern pine. With cutover pinelands of the South now regrown, G-P had begun to buy timberland there in 1960. In fact, they purchased such big chunks of pine woods as to acquire sawmills "incidentally."[22]

The Chilean economist Osvald Sunkel has written that when North American multinationals began to take control of the most dynamic industries of Latin America after World War II, they sucked "[t]he best talents that emerged from local industries. . .into the new managerial class."[23] Something like that happened at Coos Bay. Jens Jorgensen was a Coquille mill hand who used both his hands and brain to ascend the ladder into G-P management. He had an idea for making plywood out of Southern pine. G-P liked the sound of that. In early 1963, the company "literally smuggled"[24] some carloads of Southern pine to its big Coquille plywood plant. There, conducting secret nocturnal experiments with different glue formulae and drying cycles, Jorgensen found that high-grade plywood could indeed be made and mass-produced from Southern pine.

Immediately, G-P began to convert its "incidentally" acquired sawmills in the South to plywood plants. It also built new plants. With

Jorgensen's discovery for turning Southern pine into plywood, overcapacity was of no concern to G-P. The company relocated him and other West Coast managers to run their southern plywood plants. It began to gobble up additional land and companies throughout the South, which brought an outcry from the mom and pop mills, who complained to the Federal Trade Commission. In fact, the Coquille experiment resulted in a massive shift in G-P's investments. The problem for Coos Bay was that when G-P's investment went to the South, its *economy* went south.

When G-P executives later mentioned this change in the company's course, they cited the opportunity offered by the South to buy and control timberland.[25] They liked the region's good transportation network, too. And, of course, they loved the business climate: no labor unions there. Which made it possible for G-P to cut its labor costs by $1.35 an hour, on average.[26] As for the Oregon workers left behind without work, it wasn't G-P but the cutting edge of the state's pollution abatement standards that had sliced off their jobs.[27]

IN LINKING WEYCO and a hurricane a few pages back, I had in mind Hurricane Freda of 1962. Though the greatest destruction occurred well north of Coos Bay, many residents of the area have vivid memories of the Columbus Day storm, as it was known locally. Freda blew down the equivalent of an entire year's timber harvest in Washington and Oregon, including a huge volume of Weyco's Douglas fir reserves. What to do with this unlucky windfall? Weyco discovered the Japanese market for Douglas fir logs and soon became "by far" the biggest exporter of unprocessed logs from the Pacific Northwest,[28] including large volumes from its holdings near Coos Bay.

Local mills were running at capacity when the hurricane struck,[29] and the area was already exporting over sixty million board feet of logs. But, said a spokesman for a Coos Bay stevedoring firm, Japan could use "billions of board feet of logs."[30] Coos Bay-area forests would contribute heavily to Weyco's (and others') export of unprocessed logs to the Far East over succeeding decades. And speaking for the quality of the area's timber, the average value of its exported logs was higher than that of any other port in the Pacific Northwest for every year but one from 1976 to 1986.[31]

Raw log exports and the controversy attached to them weren't new. Ontario had banned log exports to the United States in 1898, inducing some U.S. lumbermen to move their manufacturing operations to the other side of the Canadian line. Luckily for places like Coos Bay, the bulkiness of logs meant that lumber manufacturers tended to build (or buy) their plants near timber supplies. (But in discussing Coos Bay's lumber industrialization in Chapter 3, I didn't mention the log experiments.) In 1884 a Coos Bay logger contracted to provide a thousand pilings and a million feet of fir logs to Pacific Lumber Company by towing them to San Francisco in a log raft. Well and good, except that heavy seas dispersed his rafts: their tug passed through the Golden Gate with nothing left to tow. I imagine these Coos Bay logs washing up on scattered beaches eventually. When they dried out, some may have fueled campfires under the blaze of tropical stars.

But other Oregon timber sites were already shipping unprocessed logs to Japan by then. In the 1890s, much too soon to represent a silent homage to Fidel Castro, an ocean log-raft specialist successfully pulled a "cigar-shaped" raft of 7,000 logs from Empire City to San Francisco.[32] So yes, it could be done. In fact, by the Depression years it was done so many times that log exports to Japan were "the only thing that kept the [Coos Bay] area in groceries."[33] Thus, there was no reason in principle to suppose that the manufacturing jobs that supported so many local workers and their families, as well as local businesses, were native to Coos Bay. No reason to think that at all.[34]

As jobs declined in the later decades of the twentieth century and log exports picked up, the exports came under mounting attack. Japan agreed to reduce log imports from the United States, but Japan, like the United States, was run by businessmen and so the agreement did not hold. Congress banned the further export of logs from federal forests on the West Coast, partially in 1968 and totally in 1974. This did not stop log exports from private timber holdings, like those of Weyco and G-P. In 1976 such exports cost an estimated 11,400 sawmill and planer-mill jobs, dwarfing "the projected unemployment which would result from the most expansive wilderness proposal."[35]

Why was Japan such a magnet for unprocessed logs from the Pacific Northwest? Well, to start with, Japanese producers had depleted much of their own country's supplies. It will be 2020 or so before the conifers of Japan's tree farms mature. Considering transportation and labor costs and comparing market prices, Pacific Northwest timber owners could net more money shipping logs to Japan than they could selling wood products in the United States. For example, in 1979 when its potential profit on lumber sales was only ten percent, Weyco lapped up a 62 percent profit on its log exports.[36]

North American logs could enter Japan duty free, but Japan penalized the import of processed wood, collecting increasing rates in proportion to value added at the exporting site. The United States does the same, allowing (for example) copper ore and bauxite to enter the country duty free and charging hefty duties on imported copper wire or aluminum. It's called protecting home industry. High tariffs on foreign manufactured goods enabled the United States to industrialize.

Japan's wood import rules served the interests of Japanese paper manufacturers at the expense of smaller sawmill operators and the mountain villagers who owned nearby forests. The latter were as upset by what they saw as unfair competition from North American logs as smaller sawmill owners and their workers in the Pacific Northwest were by Japan's buying them.[37] Exporting logs was not about exporting jobs. Jobs were eliminated in both the Pacific Northwest and in Japan. The need for transoceanic workers' solidarity was exceeded only by its absence.

ENDNOTES

1. Ross 88.

2. Robbins, *Hard Times* 134.

3. *Coos Bay Times*, April 17, 1957: 1. Cf. Ross 1980, 136.

4. Name changed to prevent any possible embarrassment.

5. See Portland *Oregonian*, April 19, 1961: 11.

6. *The World* 25 May 1961: 2.

7. *The World* 25 May 1961: 2. Cf. 15 May 1961; 17 May 1961: 1; 23 May 1961: 1; Ross 136-7.

8. Portland *Oregonian* 26 January 1981.

9. Cheatham and Pamplin 23.

10. *The World*, May 15, 1961: 5.

11. Portland *Oregonian*, April 18, 1961: 1.

12. Hidy et al. 578.

13. State of Oregon, *Department of Forestry, History of Oregon's Timber Harvests and/or Lumber Production: State Data—1849 to 1992; County Data—1925 to 1992*, compiled by Bob Bourhill (Salem: ODF, 1994) Table 22.

14. William Dietrich, *The Final Forest: The Battle for the Last Great Trees of the Pacific Northwest* (New York: Penguin, 1992) 174.

15. E.g., Robbins, *Lumberjacks and Legislators*.

16. Alexander Cockburn, "Save the Forests, or Gore?" *The Progressive Populist* 5.12 (November 15, 1999): 17.

17. *The Timberman* xlix.3 (January 1948): 35.

18. Ross 29.

19. Cheatham and Pamplin 14.

20. Ross 129 ff.

21. Ross 138.

22. Ross 165.

23. Osvald Sunkel, "Transnational Capitalism and National Disintegration in Latin America," *Social and Economic Studies* 22.1 (March 1973): 168. Witness the career with Coca Cola of Vicente Fox.

24. Cheatham and Pamplin 18.

25. Hahn 8.

26. Ross 223.

27. Ross 287-88.

28. Brian Tokar, *Earth for Sale: Reclaiming Ecology in the Age of Corporate Greenwash* (Boston: South End, 1997) 87.

29. Gordon Ross, personal interview, March 19, 2002.

30. Quoted in *The World*, April 14, 1961: 14.

31. Debra D. Warren, *Production, Prices, Employment, and Trade in Northwest Forest Industries, Second Quarter* 1987 (Portland: USDA Resource Bulletin PNW-RB-147) 25-26.

32. Beckham, *Coos Bay* 40; cf. John A. Young and Jan M. Newton, *Capitalism and Human Obsolescence: Corporate Control Versus Individual Survival in Rural America* (Montclair, N.J.: Allanheld, 1980) 23.

33. Quoted in Robbins, *Hard Times* 93. Reprinted by permission of the University of Washington Press.

34. According to one formula, every million board feet of logs milled locally created twelve full-time jobs. The same wood volume exported as logs created nine. (Gordon Ross interview.)

35. Young and Newton 37.

36. M. Patricia Marchak, *Logging the Globe* (Montreal: McGill-Queen's University Press, 1995) 76.

37. Cf. Marchak 123 ff.; "Wood Processing Industry in a 'Timber Deficit' Country, Japan: Structural Change, Adjustment Problems and Policies," United Nations Industrial Development Organization, Division of Industrial Studies, Working Paper on Structural Changes (V.83-59625: August 1983).

CHAPTER 11

The Companies Move On

WITH DEPLETION of the old-growth forests of the Pacific Northwest, smaller wood producing companies went under, while larger companies like Weyco and G-P replaced sawmills with automated processes to turn out pulp and wood chips. Log exports bypassed industrial production altogether. Much of the job loss from these developments was undramatic, almost invisible. But all too soon plant closures of the bigger companies became the subject of unsettling front-page articles.

Near Coos Bay, G-P closed its veneer plant in Powers, one-time hub of Coos Bay Lumber's logging operations. Without notice, 150 workers lost their jobs and Powers lost a third of its population. Eight years later, in the summer of 1979, the G-P job ax struck again. It fell on workers at the company's Coos Bay plywood plant, its second largest in the state. Some of the 230 employees thrown out of work had worked there for two decades. They learned of the closure at the end of their shift.

Asked about the shutdown, G-P vice president George Ritchie gave the following rationale. The plant was designed to receive old-growth logs, which came to it via the estuary. The smaller second-growth logs now available would have had to be brought in "by land"—that is, by filling in the bay. In other words, the remaining logs were too small to make up a log raft! No wonder old-timers called them "pecker poles."[1] The only other thing G-P could do, Ritchie sought to explain, would be to bid on the old-growth timber of public forests. Either way, continued operations at Coos Bay would be too expensive for the company.[2]

Over the following months, G-P closed its Coos Bay resins plant, its veneer plant, and its hardboard operation. By then hard times were not confined to Coos Bay. The Federal Reserve's high interest rates had thrown the national economy into a deep, dark place. Manufactured goods from the Douglas fir region could no longer compete with those of lower cost, wood-products areas, such as Canada and the South. With profit margins in tatters, Oregon producers closed mills, cut wages in reopened mills, hired non-union workers, and continued to substitute machinery for workers to gain greater productivity. But, again, it was the situation at Coos Bay that was "a cautionary example" to the region. And no wonder: seven out of ten Coos Bay-area jobs were timber-related, the highest proportion in the state.[3]

Meanwhile, G-P did all right. Sales climbed throughout the nation's economic slump, although by 1983 the corporation had 5,000 fewer employees than it had had in 1979. Yet, at the beginning of the downturn, G-P's Robert Flowerree had declared, "We consider our employees our most valuable resource."[4] Evidently the company's most valuable resource was also its most expendable.

By the early 1980s, G-P had become the leading plywood producer in the United States, thanks in large part to the Jorgensen experiment discussed Chapter 10. Company headquarters tagged behind corporate investments, moving to Atlanta in 1982. Two years earlier the company had closed the last of its Oregon lumber mills, although in 1994 G-P started a scaled-down sawmill operation at Coos Bay. G-P had also become the world's largest owner of timberland, with nine million acres. As for the Coquille plywood plant that had served as a launching pad for G-P's rocket to the South, G-P shut it down in 1991, throwing 320 employees out of work.

However, G-P was not alone in responding to timber depletion in the Pacific Northwest by moving to the South. Weyco and others played the same card, drawn there "at least in part, [by] the relative permissiveness of the South, where most forests are in private. . .hands, and where logging is subject to few regulations." No wonder southern "softwood cutting now exceeds replanting" and, according to a U.S. Forest Service report, southern hardwoods "face a similar fate."[5]

One particular G-P closure deserves attention here. In 1980 the company quit production at its Coos Bay hardboard plant, built by Coos Bay Lumber in 1949. G-P spokesman George Richie explained that new technology and the closure of other mills had diminished the supply of waste materials used to manufacture hardboard. This baffled hardboard expert Armin Wehrle. Although unprofitable in the short term because of the wounded economy, the plant was viable in the long . Supplies were available and its product was marketable.[6] But G-P had another hardboard plant in Virginia.

In other words, G-P workers at Coos Bay were competing with G-P workers in the South. And the Coos Bay workers had proven too costly, in G-P's view. Just as the Coquille plywood workers who participated in the Jorgensen experiment helped eliminate future jobs in Coquille, G-P distilled the sweat of workers at Coos Bay and throughout the Pacific Northwest to finance the transfer of their jobs to the South and some places even more remote. As one commentator laconically said, "since some companies are investing in manufacturing plants elsewhere, they must be removing profits made in declining regions."[7]

WEYCO BEGAN REDUCING local payrolls in 1979. In January 1984, the company closed the gates on the remaining 200 workers at its Coos Bay plywood plant. In January 1989, the company announced the closure of its sawmill in North Bend, ending thirty-seven years of continuous operation at "the area's last big mill"[8] and laying off the remaining workforce there of about 200. Weyco also shut down operations at its Allegany logging site, an 88,000-acre segment of its Millicoma holdings. In the words of local reporter John Griffith, a former worker there, "Now all cut and logged, the tree farm is growing another crop" of trees.[9] While it was busy doing that, a crop of unpaid bills was flourishing in the homes of workers and their families at Coos Bay.

The top five Weyco executives received almost $2.9 million in cash compensation for the year the company closed the North Bend sawmill down. Well over a third of it went to George H. Weyerhaeuser. His choice of parents had been very wise.

When I asked a company spokesman why Weyco had closed the North Bend mill, he said that Weyco's plan had been to harvest the old-growth timber on its private lands, then harvest old-growth timber that it got from public lands, then return to regrown private stocks. However, the environmental concerns that led to public timber set-asides had given this plan the bird—specifically, the northern spotted owl. "With that resource [i.e. public timber] tied up, there was no place to go for logs,"[10] said the Weyco rep. And the North Bend mill was geared to process old-growth logs. What about his company's pledge of 1961 to provide "an uninterrupted and endless timber supply" from its vast arboreal farm? I was too polite to ask.

In any case, Weyco had thrown Coos Bay something more than a bone. At the time that the company announced its biggest local closures, Weyco also announced conversion of a former G-P operation into a "mill of the '90s." Coos Bay Export (CBX) was specifically designed to turn second-growth Douglas fir into metrically cut posts and beams for export to Japan. By 1991 CBX employed 125 workers on three shifts. This invites comparison with the 1,500 or so who had worked at the North Bend operation at times, but it was certainly better than no jobs at all.

In late 1997, the corporate millipede dropped its last remaining local shoe, which fell with a thud that was an echo of the Asian currency collapse. Japan's middle class could no longer afford American-style homes. In addition to the loss of jobs, the demise of CBX delivered an additional blow to Coos Bay, as Weyco's export mill had brought the area the cargo trade of a major shipping line. Now that was gone, too.[11]

Weyco also sold its old-growth North Bend mill site to the Coquille Indians for conversion into a casino, providing a well-deserved source of revenue for descendants of the tribes which formerly had their villages along the upper and lower Coquille. They were mutual enemies then, by some accounts.[12] Amalgamated, they had struck a favorable deal with the white man.

SPEAKING AT THE SOCIETY of Foresters' annual symposium of 1991, which was held at Coos Bay, a university professor waxed nostalgic about the importance of the now departed lumber mills to the region's timber communities. "Besides being the economic base," he told his audience, "the mills were the focal point around which the community revolved."[13] One former mill has become the center of renewed activity. Inspired by the same jackpot hopes that brought members of the Coos Bay Commercial Company to Coos Bay in the first place, the crowd that frequents the Mill Resort & Casino, located in the cavernous spaces of what was Weyco's old-growth sawmill, makes it the busiest spot on the bay. But the focus is on the cards, the slots, the bingo calls. Only a Casino booster would call the place a focal point for community.

But what about the irony of a site where people formerly earned a living being turned into a place where they can pour their earnings into a collecting device? Of course, they no doubt sometimes win, or some of them do, at least.

LIKE G-P, WEYCO RENEGED on its deal with Coos Bay. Local residents had "kept inviolate" their end of the bargain, just as the Coosans had. They provided the companies with a steady stream of workers, men and women who were as good as any at the work they did. More than that, the corporate giants got to "farm" an area amounting to almost a third of the county's surface, taking out a substantial portion of the area's ancient forest. Sadly, they did so with enthusiastic local support. Even when Weyco closed its North Bend mill, the mayor polished the lock on the gate by explaining that the company was making a transition from old-growth to harvesting "second- and third-growth plantation trees."[14] A *transition*! To my mind, Weyco's "transition" had left Coos Bay in the lurch.

Of course, no soldiers would appear to evict the displaced workers and their families from Coos Bay. They would not be marched off to a reservation up the coast. But thousands who remained where they were would find that they had lost a good part of their reason for living there, and the area would begin to die.

Just as other kinds of extractive firms move elsewhere with the exhaustion of soil or mines, companies like Weyco and G-P respond to forest depletion by opening operations in other, untapped and increasingly remote, areas. As early as the mid-1970s, George Weyerhaeuser told the New York Society of Security Analysts that his company had "freed" itself of its West Coast enterprises, acquiring "major Indonesian operations" to go with its 700,000 acres of timber cutting rights in Borneo and the Philippines.[15] By 1978 Weyco held title to extensive acreage in the South and cutting rights to 10.7 million acres worldwide. Already "the world's largest producer of softwood lumber and market pulp" at the end of the century, Weyco's 1999 acquisition of the Canadian giant MacMillan Bloedel was expected to boost corporate sales from $10.8 billion to $13.3 billion a year.[16] Despite coloring itself ever greener,[17] Weyco has "taken up the mass export of logs from Siberia, where clearcuts of forest habitat threaten extinction for the Siberian tiger."[18] Although the company has not entirely "freed" itself of operations in the Pacific Northwest, its logging crews in that unhappy area are cutting smaller and smaller trees.

G-P is following a similarly globalized course but with a surprising twist. For many years "one of the largest landowners in the nation,"[19] G-P was planning to sell all of its U.S. timberland, as of December 2000. Henceforth, the company would buy what logs it needed on the market and focus its vast synergies on the production of consumer goods, especially paper products. While the corporation's switch to recession-proof products, such as toilet paper, was nothing new, its projected sale of timberland was a major shift and "not without [internal] controversy."[20] But the company retains plenty of timberland in other parts of the world. Closer to home, G-P can always buy some timber-owning companies, should the need arise. In 2001 it did just that, adding Plum Creek Timber Company to the corporate spin-off which it calls The Timber Company.

BIG TIMBER IS A PART of a free trade regime in which national boundaries mean less and less. In 1992 when Weyco was the leading U.S. exporter of forest products, much of its Canadian production was exported *to* the U.S. In 2001, instead of joining smaller U.S. producers, who charge Canada with dumping its wood products on the United States, and environmentalists, who fear for Canada's unprotected forests, Weyco's CEO wrote a letter to the respective heads of state offering to initiate mediation to resolve this U.S.-Canadian trade dispute. Why not? The company's multinational interests transcend those of Canada or the United States. Or was it just that Weyco couldn't afford to let U.S. producers win?[21] The corporate executive who dreamed of buying an island and moving his headquarters there so as to make his company "beholden to no nation"[22] was just a little ahead of his time.

Just as Weyco only nominally remains a U.S. firm, a future wood products industry at Coos Bay could be managed by companies based in Canada, Japan, Sweden, or elsewhere outside the United States. Would Coos Bay residents be any worse off?

With Coos Bay's mills shut down, the volume of log exports from the area jumped in 1982, and then it jumped some more. Timber owners didn't have to wait for their trees to mature when they were selling them for pulp. Log exports continued "to be a major factor in the local economy" at the end of that cruel decade.[23] When I returned to the area recently, the stacks of logs along the bay had grown considerably from what I'd seen two years before. It was as though a sorcerer's apprentice with a chainsaw had run amok in Coos Bay's last remaining woods. Former County Commissioner Gordon Ross explained that logs are towed down the coast from as far north as Alaska, then deposited at Coos Bay to await truck transfer to manufacturing plants along the "I-5 corridor" of Oregon's interior. One-time Coos Bay manufacturers have become log brokers, said another source.

Coos Bay's industrialization had been a by-product of investment by remotely based capitalists. They piled up the area's wealth for themselves, and they were the ones who benefited from the adoption of more effective production processes. When it served their interests to extract the remainder of Coos Bay's timber without local processing, they didn't hesitate to "undevelop" Coos Bay.

ENDNOTES

1. Robbins, *Hard Times* 122. Reprinted by permission of the University of Washington Press.

2. Church, "G-P's Coos Bay pullout blamed on varied factors," Portland *Oregonian*, January 26, 1981.

3. Robbins, "Timber Town: Market Economics in Coos Bay, Oregon, 1850 to the Present," *Pacific Northwest Quarterly* 75.4 (October 1984): 154.

4. Georgia-Pacific 1979 Annual Report (Portland: G-P) 16.

5. *San Francisco Chronicle* 8 August 2000: A5.

6. Church, "G-P's Coos Bay pullout."

7. Marchak 43.

8. *The World*, January 17, 1989: 1.

9. *The World*, January 4, 1989.

10. Paul Barnum, Weyerhaeuser's public affairs representative in Oregon, email to the author, December 4, 1998.

11. Gordon Ross, personal interview.

12. See, e.g., Beckham, *The Indians* 95-96.

13. *The World*, May 10, 1991: 1.

14. *The World*, January 5, 1989.

15. Young and Newton 53.

16. *San Francisco Chronicle*, June 22, 1999.

17. Visit the company's web page at<http://www.Weyerhaeuser.com>; cf. Tokar 20.

18. John Trumpbour, "Greenwash and Globalization," rev. of *The Corporate Planet* by Joshua Karliner, *Monthly Review* 50.10 (March 1999): 55.

19. *New York Times*, October 25, 1970.

20. Stace Gordon, telephone interview, December 28, 2000.

21. But for now they have. In August 2001, the Bush administration announced a retroactive 19.3 percent penalty on U.S. imports of Canadian softwood lumber. *San Francisco Chronicle* August 11, 2001: A5. Four months later, according to an American Lands Alliance press release of December 18, 2001, a British Columbian lumber company sued the U.S. for $250 million under Chapter 11 of the North American Free Trade Agreement (NAFTA). Weyco has now (May 2002) joined other companies in filing a NAFTA challenge against the U.S.

22. Quoted in Giovanni Arrighi, *The Long Twentieth Century: Money, Power, and the Origins of Our Times* (New York: Verso, 1994) 82. The entire quote should be read. Cf. former General Electric CEO Jack Welch's reply to the question of where might be the best place for a company to operate. "On a barge," he said. Quoted by Charles Kernaghan on Flashpoints, KPFA, Berkeley, March 26, 2002.

23. *The World*, January 18, 1989.

CHAPTER 12

Left Behind

I

THE BIG WOOD-PRODUCT MAKERS didn't leave a vacuum when they vacated Coos Bay. Besides the casino and the rusting shells of closed-down manufacturing plants, they left behind a lot of shattered hopes and lives. They also left a lingering urge to blame. Trees or jobs: that had been the choice according to the industry reps, their academic backers, and the media. Places like Coos Bay had had the wrong choice made for them.

But what kind of choice was that? If you were a laid-off Coos Bay mill worker with a family to support, the last thing you wanted to hear was that the lives of trees and the animals that lived in them were more important than the lives of you and your family. As the wife of one such person argued in a letter to the editor of Coos Bay's *The World* (headed "Don't let owls take precedence"), "I am for saving animals from being extinct, but not when they take precedence over human beings."[1] Humans had to come first. The environmentalists had everything upside down. Without their appeals of public timber sales, there would be a lot more timber to cut, and with that timber cut, a lot more jobs. A 1989 ruling by a Portland judge led to timber harvest cutbacks on land near Coos Bay, among other sites.[2] Pacific Coast mill owners were saying that such litigation could result in the loss of 16,000 jobs.[3]

Why were people out to save the trees anyway? If they weren't logged, the trees would die a useless death. So said another letter to the editor.[4] Besides everything else, there was no good reason to believe the so-called experts when they said that we were nearly out of trees, for "we can see millions of acres of trees everywhere we drive in the Pacific Northwest."[5] Such views were common at Coos Bay and other timber towns.

It was the fault of the government, people said, the National

Forest Service. The bureaucrats had created an "artificial timber short-age" by choking off supplies. What the government should have been doing was making up the gap between the industry's used-up old growth and its maturing second and third growth.[6] Government bureaucrats were, of course, an easy target. It must have seemed to most people, and rightly so, that the government had done little for them in a long, long time. The government only seemed to do things *to* them, such as holding back a serious chunk of their hard-earned pay. Whose timber was it anyway? The national forest timber wasn't really the government's. It belonged to everyone, and (as one letter to the editor urged) the federal land "should be administered for the benefit of all the people of our nation,"[7] and not just environmentalists.

Besides creating a shortage of logs and, thereby, jobs, restricted public timber sales had other effects. Under federal law, the state allocates a portion of the proceeds from such sales to local school districts and public works.[8] But why should the sale of public timber affect school children? Clearly the point of such legislation is to make sure that local communities have a vested interest in higher levels of public timber harvests. The children serve as hostages.

With the government, at least there was something that people could do. They could write their letters to the editor or, better yet, to their political representatives. They could go to the state capitol. If you were a logger you could drive your vehicle to the capitol, and if enough of you did that, you could make a rolling, honking picket line of logging trucks around that capitol building. In January 2001, a California man used his truck as a petition, revving it up to high speed and driving it directly into the state's capitol building, leaving the state with substantial property damage and himself with his brains dashed out. His anger must have spoken to many up and down the coast and wherever else his death became a news item, even though it didn't stem from timber set-asides. Here's hoping that his choice of political tactics fell on deaf ears.

But people knew, or at least they thought they did, who the real enemy was. It was the environmentalist, cruising through the area with his radical bumper stickers and his California license plates. Nothing better to do than try to get the government to lock off valuable timber, when there was "already more [of it] to see than any working person would ever have to time to see."[9] The local newspaper called the common enemy "intellectual irresponsibles" and "wolves on the prowl." These "various people, some completely unemployed, others professing certain avocations," were never up to any good.[10] Having too much time on their hands, they were like the devil who, having nothing better to do, devoured his children.

The editor was playing on the ancient harp of prejudice against people who don't have to make a living with their backs and hands. He ended his diatribe on a tremulous note: "When will the working stiffs ever count in this state?"

When I thought about the personal implications of these letters to the editor and the anti-environmentalist editorials, I felt a little uncomfortable. *I* drove a car with California plates. *I* used to work for the government. Since I was retired, *I* was "completely unemployed." *And* I had avocational interests. I was no tree hugger, but as a card-carrying member of the Sierra Club, I might give one a pat now and then.

Again, I had to recognize the fact that Coos Bay and I had gone our different ways. My childhood in North Bend counted for nothing around there. I felt fortunate that my family had moved away, but that had made it easier for me to turn to my memories than return to Coos Bay.

Also, I couldn't help remembering Murray Bookchin's argument about the working class becoming industrialized instead of radicalized, becoming the counterpart instead of the opponent of the bourgeoisie.[11] Workers who identified with timber owners' objectives were not going to become a "revolutionary force" any time soon. Still, Coos Bay's longshoremen of the 1930s had acted on awareness of their interest as a separate and antagonistic class.

FOR ALL THE FINGERS pointing at environmentalists, forest ecosystems were not the only beneficiaries of the Endangered Species Act and its judicial support. As William Dietrich has pointed out, "locking up publicly owned timber on national forests to protect the spotted owl is not a dire threat" to giant timber owners.[12] For them, the environmental set-asides both wiped out the competition of smaller mills and raised the value of their own holdings. As Weyco et al. saw things, there was "an historical oversupply of sawmills."[13] The industry needed a good shaking out. One reason for the industrial giants' buying up timberland in Indonesia, Malaysia, South Korea, Canada, and elsewhere for decades past was to ensure that they did not get caught without any trees to cut.

Here was a further irony. By 1988, demand for fir and other

131

woods had shot up higher than the tallest redwood tree. Where there were still big trees to log, reopened sawmills were breaking production records, and this despite record exports of unprocessed logs. Oregon was harvesting 13 percent more timber than it had a decade earlier, yet there were fewer jobs than in the 1970s, when the workforce was already getting pinched. *Cutting more trees was not providing more jobs.* How could this be? Could it have something to do with the fact that machines were doing more of the work than ever before?

Producers had come out of the devastating recession of the early 1980s into a big, new globalized world of competition from lower cost areas, such as Canada and the South. They responded as producers do under such circumstances, by trying to cut their own production costs. The corporate giants did this by shifting investments to the less expensive sites. The smaller producers tried to increase their workers' productivity. For those who still had jobs, this could mean production speed-ups, longer hours, and intensified work. For employers, it mainly meant investing in machinery to do more of the work. A federal study showed that "modernization" of plants, not timber set-asides or log exports, was "the biggest threat to timber industry jobs."[14] With fewer jobs on offer and a non-union workforce becoming the norm, the entire industry had become "increasingly slimmed-down."[15]

With such increased productivity, manufacturing plants turned out more wood products than even a hungry market could digest. The old bogey of overproduction again raised its ugly head. Remaining workers found its gaze as potent as their predecessors had a hundred years before. Soon they were stuck at home again or standing in the unemployment line. At Coos Bay, Weyco offered its remaining employees a choice between their jobs and the existing union contract. The workers made the choice they had to make, but Weyco closed its North Bend mill all the same. One environmentalist, his back to the wall, urged employers to remain competitive by installing more labor-saving machinery![16]

As economist Doug Dowd has said, "the relationship between the powerful and the relatively powerless has never been one of honesty."[17] In his landmark decision of 1991, putting a hold on timber sales on 66,000 acres of U.S. Forest Service land, U.S. Judge William Dwyer declared that "Job losses in the wood products industry will continue regardless of whether the northern spotted owl is protected." The leading factor that he cited in support of this conclusion was the "modernization of physical plants."[18] But the story usually told in the media and on the street said little about the "quiet revolution"[19] that resulted in job losses despite more timber being cut.

The new economy's revolution in information technology has put financial services in a position to orchestrate a "global dispersal of productive processes and sites."[20] If only workers could reach across boundaries as easily. But they cannot, and the hyper-mobility of capital has brought changes in the geography of industrial work. As Arif Dirlik has said:

> Parts of the earlier Third World are today in the pathways of transnational capital and belong in the "developed" sector of the world economy. Likewise, parts of the First World, marginalized in the new global economy, are hardly distinguishable in way of life from what used to be viewed as Third World characteristics.[21]

Coos Bay's union-scale work in mills and on the docks has for now been replaced by McJobs: temp work, cashiering, retail sales, food service (which alone now offers more jobs than do lumber and wood products[22]), and jobs in convalescent homes. Then there are the 346 people whose work was featured in a recent *New York Times* article ("Paul Bunyan Settling into His New Cubicle"). These workers earn $8 to $9 an hour at an "office park" in North Bend. How? By doing telephone tech support for a Virginia-based firm. Local officials were reportedly "thrilled to have landed a high-tech company."[23]

De-industrialized, Coos Bay has entered the information age—but only as a source of cheap labor and, of course, consumption of goods from the more "developed" parts of the world.

II

TO GIVE THE LUMBER COMPANIES their due, they also left behind them at Coos Bay a future timber "crop." Before considering the implications, let's glance at the history of this phenomenon. Replanting in logged off and otherwise barren areas goes back to Arbor Day, if not before. But the main players in the industry did not cotton to reforesting, even when they found that clear-cut land in the Pacific Northwest was used up land. They couldn't sell it to farmers, as they had planned, but regrowing timber didn't make any money for the firm. George S. Long, a star of Weyco management in the company's formative years, recognized that the leading softwood species of the Pacific Northwest needed decades to reach commercial maturity. *Several* decades. He thought that the government should buy and replant the cutover areas. As late as 1923, the president of the National Lumber Manufacturers Association could bleat that it would be "absurd to reproduce trees that would be realized only by a man's grandchildren."[24] Let the grandkids look out for themselves!

Two years later, one company, at least, was starting to listen to academic crooners such as G.W. Peavy when they sang, "The forest is a crop."[25] A crop! Weyco began to experiment with replanting and selective logging. I'll not attempt to answer here the question of whether the company was more concerned with protecting its huge investment in timberland or its public image. Certainly the industry had come under heavy fire for its traditional tactics of cut and run. What is clear is that by 1937 Weyco had started a public relations campaign to color itself green. "Timber is a crop," its ads proclaimed, though it was not until 1941 that the company seeded its first tree farm.

Within another five years, Weyco had a dozen tree farms, plus a share in two more. The company was heading "toward forest industrialization," as a Weyco V.P. proudly said.[26] Other members of the industry had fallen into line by then, and there were thousands of such farms. As a toddler, G-P was a little slow to catch on. "[T]here will always be an adequate supply of American timber," argued a Georgia-Hardwood publication c. 1943, because "timber is a self-perpetuating crop."[27] Just leave it alone and nature would replace the trees you cut. But nature's way was slow. Discovering that it could grow four or five trees for every one it harvested, G-P started replanting logged-off areas, too.

LET ME SAY SOMETHING here about the slogan "timber is a crop." Its root assumption is that the forest consists of an extractable resource—namely, timber—which is marketable trees. Already we have come a long, long way from Coosan awe and reverence. But mainly "timber is a crop" declares that timber has more in common with farm produce than it does with minerals. The woods are more like wheat than iron ore. Unlike minerals, under proper conditions and with enough time, timber will indeed replace itself. Executives of Weyco and G-P have loved to point this out. Wood, they say, is "a renewable organic resource,"[28] the only self-replacing one.[29]

Problems? For one, the average Douglas fir lives for over 500 years, given half a chance. But it is unprofitable for timber companies to allow their trees to grow for more than around fifty years, even though (as Dietrich says) the point at which a Douglas fir should be cut "to produce the most amount of added fiber per year is after eighty or one hundred years, not fifty."[30] But again, investors can't expect to live as long as their grandchildren.

In the 1960s Weyco decided it could further outdo Mother Nature by combining genetically screened seedlings, heavy chemical sprayings, and liberal dosages of fertilizer to create "a truly managed forest." Their test-tube forest would produce much greater biomass—ultimately, much greater profit —than a wild forest ever could.[31]

Once more, other companies followed Weyco's lead, spraying seeds by helicopter, hand-planting seedlings, speeding growth with the equivalent of antibiotics and steroids. Big Timber turned huge sections of natural woodlands into something like a farm, but a factory farm. D.H. Lawrence's indictment perfectly anticipated these men who would "produce a mental cunning and mechanical force that would outwit Nature and chain her down completely, completely, till at last there should be nothing free. . .at all, all should be controlled, domesticated, put to man's meaner uses."[32]

But as Chris Maser has declared, "the forest is not a machine."[33] Destroying the interrelated processes and biological diversity of the Pacific Northwest's native forests and replacing them with monotypical plantations fed by increasing amounts of fertilizers, herbicides, and pesticides is a vast experiment. Its long-term outcomes for ecosystems, local communities, future generations, and even for the wood produced cannot be known.[34]

Were biological instead of economic motives driving forestry, we might put old-growth logging on a cycle of 350 years, an interval adopted by the Bureau of Land Management on some of its southwestern Oregon acreage.[35] But for members of the Big Timber club, biological considerations must be made to serve the bottom line.

ACCOMPANYING ONE OF THE editorial attacks on environmentalists that I came across in Coos Bay's newspaper was an article on another page headed, "Expert says trees talk with waves." It seems that an electrical engineer had recorded electrical impulses emitted by trees. When cut they "put out a tremendous cry of alarm." The "adjacent trees put out smaller ones."[36]

Besides undercutting the point of the editorial, the article gave me pause for thought. If trees could cry out in pain, maybe they could talk. What might a tree in a managed forest have to say for itself and its thousands of identical sibs? Would it brag about their accelerated rate of growth? Complain about the missing brush and logs? Bemoan the prospect of their premature demise? What about the chemicals sprayed on them and their effect, as run-off, on the downstream fish? But I'll let an unnamed southerner have the final word on this, instead of a Franken-Tree. Pondering a twenty by seven foot chunk of Douglas fir in a touring environmentalist display, he observed, "It's all been cut down here and there's not even a damn squirrel in these woods."[37] By "these woods," he must have had in mind the region's rigid rows of plantation pines. Such plantations now occupy 40 percent of the coastal pine forest of the southeastern U.S.[38]

CLEARLY, COOS BAY'S major problems turned on the lag time between timber crops. The companies that logged off the old growth much faster than they could replace it were responding to market and financial pulls. The promise of sustainable production went by the boards. Two generations of Coos Bay workers would have been no worse off as miners of depleted ore. Two generations and counting. . .

Displaced local workers have no choice but to try to adjust to early, forced retirement or to lower earnings in some other line of work. They don't have the time to wait for second- or third-growth timber to reach some minimal level of commercial maturity. Nor do investors, "if they have alternatives."[39] And they *do* have alternatives. For example, a company may forgo any attempt to hold trees in reserve for even fifty years, harvesting smaller trees at frequent intervals instead for pulp and low-quality lumber.

In what may prove an ominous trend for Coos Bay, the nexus of corporate ownership, clear-cutting of old growth, captive governments, mass production, and global marketing has gone globally south, establishing new plantations of fast-growing pines and eucalyptuses in Brazil, Chile, Iberia, New Zealand, Australia, Indonesia, and other areas offering favorable growing conditions and juicy cost advantages. What grows faster than a eucalyptus? Not much. They grow like weeds, and their droppings suffocate competing growth. All in all, the eucalyptus is a pulp marketer's dream. Thailand's enormous eucalyptus plantations are "harvested like so many rows of corn."[40] Meanwhile, in northern Oregon the pulp of hybrid poplars will allegedly take pressure off of old-growth Douglas fir.

Plantations of one particular species, mainly in Europe and New Zealand, hold a special irony for residents of Coos Bay. I mean *Chamaecyparis lawsoniana*, the Port Orford cedar, also known as white cedar and the Lawson cypress. Such trees were Coos Bay natives: their range was pretty much limited to about 200 miles of the coastal forest extending south. Though my father liked to identify trees as we sped by in the family car, I don't recall his ever pointing out a white cedar. Read on and you will understand why.

While building a brig in 1857, Asa Simpson discovered that the "aromatic and pliant" wood of *Chamaecyparis lawsoniana* was "the best material on the Coast" for building ships.[41] It was impervious to acids, termites, and shipworms, and, thought Simpson, there was plenty of it too. But others were also discovering the unique properties of this "magnificent tree." While Simpson was experimenting with its shipbuilding qualities, H.H. Luse was gaining a "near monopoly" of production and export of white cedar lumber at Coos Bay. But Simpson and the others soon caught up.[42]

By 1874 local mills were paying at least three times as much for Port Orford cedar logs as they paid for those of Douglas fir. And this was before an eight-year boom in the cedar's price. Pacific coast match factories would use nothing else, despite its value as material for finishing and furniture. A former customs collector at Empire City in the 1880s saw cargoes of half a million board feet bound for San Francisco and resale to match factories for fifteen to twenty dollars a cord—"and not a knot in the whole cargo."[43]

Strong demand for white cedar and its products continued into the twentieth century. During World War I, manufacturers used it in making airplanes. Acid-proof, the cedar served as raw material for production in a bevy of battery separator plants. North Bend had a Port Orford Cedar Manufacturing Company. The Japanese favored it for building shrines. They took in 30 percent of the 50 million feet of cedar logs produced in 1922, when "Port Orford white cedar [had also] been the big item in the lumber business of Coos County during the [previous] year."[44]

There was a catch to this—and it shouldn't come as a surprise. A 1922 trade journal article by a U.S. forester explained that Port Orford cedar, already greatly depleted, tended to be scattered throughout the forest rather than growing in pure stands. Selected for their market value, they were often cut before Douglas fir. Subsequently, new cedar growth would be destroyed when Douglas fir was logged. Clearcutting offered the best possibility for "natural" regrowth—that is, from cones. But squirrels preferred the seeds of Douglas fir. If a fire destroyed all but rodent-stored seeds, as fires sometimes did, new growth would be limited to Douglas firs.[45] But the point is clear: the most valuable of the area's big trees was also the most vulnerable.

Surrounding the forester's warning are full-page ads by the producers of Port Orford cedar logs, lumber, and other products. We may judge their effectiveness by the fact that in 1935 another U.S. forester would warn of "an appalling tragedy about to take place"[46]—namely, the exhaustion of Port Orford cedar within the next quarter century. By 1993 white cedar logs exported from Coos Bay had the highest value of any species shipped from ports in the Pacific Northwest, well over twice that of Douglas fir.[47] In fact, "thanks to past overexploitation," the Port Orford cedar "is now the most valuable wood harvested in western North America."[48]

What the chainsaw hasn't done, a fungus introduced by human contact has. It rots the roots, killing the tree in all its ages and throughout its natural habitat. A cure has not been found. "Of all major forest trees found in western North America," a pair of specialists concludes, "this species has suffered most from human activity."[49]

But what about those Port Orford cedar plantations mentioned at the start? Well, their owners mainly cultivate the tree for sale as an ornamental plant, suitable for hedges or for individual plantings "of either full-sized or dwarfed varieties."[50] "Full-sized?" I doubt it. Left to itself the tree can grow up to 300 feet in height. But I almost forgot: cultivators also sell the branches of the "Lawson cypress" (as it's now usually called) for use in floral displays. As in: "Would you like to add some greenery to your bouquet?"

ENDNOTES

1. *The World*, May 25, 1991: 4.

2. An Oregon congressman blamed budgetary fumbling by the Bureau of Land Management, not environmentalists, for these reductions. See "BLM policy blasted" in *The World*, February 18, 1989.

3. "Mill owners see massive layoffs." *The World*, January 21, 1989.

4. From Carl Bay, *The World*, May 27, 1991: 4.

5. Louis Pribble, letter, *The World*, May 22, 1991: 4.

6. Barney Dowdle and Steve H. Hanke in *Forestlands: Public and Private*, eds. Robert T. Deacon and M. Bruce Johnson (Cambridge, Mass.: Ballinger, 1985) 92.

7. Mark W. Villers, letter, *The World*, February 6, 1989: 4.

8. Gordon Ross, personal interview.

9. Villers 4.

10. *The World*, February 11, 1989.

11. In Murray Bookchin, *Remaking Society: Pathways to a Green Future* (Boston: South End, 1990) 132. Cf. the account of an auto assembly-line worker in Ben Hamper, *Rivethead: Tales From the Assembly Line* (New York: Warner, 1986).

12. Dietrich 122.

13. Dietrich 123; cf. Weyerhaeuser Co. Annual Report for 1991: 10.

14. Cited in editorial, *The World*, February 28, 1989.

15. Mary Lou Corlett, ed., *Forest Industries 1988–89 North American Factbook* (San Francisco: Miller Freeman, 1988) 1.

16. *The World*, January 21, 1989.

17. In Doug Dowd, *Blues for America: a Critique, a Lament, and Some Memories* (New York: Monthly Review Press, 1997) 285.

18. Quoted in Dietrich, 264.

19. Michael Sullivan, "Oregon's Forest Industry," *Assessment of Oregon's Forests: A Collection of Papers*, ed. Gary J. Lettman (Salem, Ore.: Oregon DOF, 1988) 162.

20. Hardt and Negri 297; cf. 280 ff.

21. From Arif Dirlik, *After the Revolution: Waking to Global Capitalism* 52, ©1994 by Arif Dirlik and reprinted by permission of Wesleyan University Press.

22. State of Oregon, Employment Department, "Coos Bay/Gold Beach Labor Trends: September 1998," compiled by John Anderson, Regional Economist (Salem, Ore.: OED, 1998) 4.

23. Sam Howe Verhovek, "Paul Bunyan Settling Into His Cubicle," *New York Times*, August 21, 2000: A14. Article begins on A1.

24. Quoted in Robbins, *Lumberjacks and Legislators* 105.

25. Peavy, "Perpetual Forest Industry in Oregon," *The Timberman* xxiii.5 (March 1922): 139.

26. Edmund Hayes, as quoted. in *The Timberman* xlix.9 (July 1948): 84.

27. *Wedge, Sr.* 67.

28. George H. Weyerhaeuser, *"Forests for the Future": the Weyerhaeuser Story* (New York: The Newcomen Society, 1981) 21.

29. Cheatham and Pamplin 9.

30. Dietrich 129. Cf. John Bellamy Foster, "Ecology Against Capitalism," *Monthly Review* 53.5 (October 2001): 4, who says, "The short-term time horizon endemic to capitalist investment decisions becomes a critical factor in determining its overall environmental effects."

31. Dietrich 125; cf. G. Weyerhaeuser 18.

32. D.H. Lawrence, *Etruscan Places* in *D.H. Lawrence and Italy* (New York: Penguin, 1985) 75.

33. Chris Maser, "A Sustainable Forest," *Assessment* 127; see also Orin Langelle, "From Native Forest to Frankenforest" in *Redesigning Life? The Worldwide Challenge to Genetic Engineering,* ed. Brian Tokar (New York: Zed, 2001).

34. Nor can we know the long-term effects of genetically altering trees. See Native Forest Network, *From Native Forests to Franken-Trees* (Burlington, Vt.: NFN, 2001).

35. *The World,* May 29, 1981.

36. Quoted in *The World,* February 11, 1989.

37. Quoted in Dietrich 152.

38. Langelle 120.

39. Marchak 34.

40. Mark Hertsgaard, *Earth Odyssey: Around the World in Search of Our Environmental Future* (New York: Broadway, 1998) 88.

41. Beckham, *Coos Bay* 29; Simpson, Dictation to Sessions, January 29, 1890 (Berkeley: Bancroft Collection) 12-13. The fragrance of wood from the Port Orford cedar, which is really a cypress, reminded some of roses, but the smell was so potent that mill workers were reportedly weakened by exposure to it and sometimes had to switch to handling other kinds of wood. See *Coos Bay News,* December 18, 1881.

42. Cox, "Lumber and Ships" 19.

43. C.B. Watson, *Prehistoric Siskiyou Island and Marble Halls of Oregon* (Ashland, Ore.: n.p. 1909) 100.

44. *The Timberman* xxiii.4 (February 1922): 64.

45. See J.V. Hofmann, "Port Orford Cedar and Selective Logging," *The Timberman* xxiii.6 (April 1922): 66-70.

46. Quoted in Robbins, *Hard Times* 128. Reprinted by permission of the University of Washington Press.

47. Warren, *Production, Prices, Employment, and Trade in Northwest Forest Industries, First Quarter 1993* (Portland: USDA Resource Bulletin PNW-RB-198) 42.

48. Christopher J. Earle and M. P. Frankis, eds., "*Chamaecyparis lawsoniana* (A. Murray) Parlatore 1864," <http://www.conifers.org/index.htm>.

49. Earle and Frankis.

50. Donald B. Zobel, "*Chamaecyparis lawsoniana* (A. Murr.) Parl.—Port Orford Cedar," <http://willow.ncfes.umn. edu/silvics_manual/Volume_1/chamaecyparis lawsoniana.htm>.

CHAPTER 13

The Road Ahead

COULD THINGS have turned out differently at Coos Bay? What if the local communities had owned the timber growing there? The idea is not so far-fetched: Mexican communal farming associations (*ejidos*) own 80 percent of that country's native forests;[1] thousands of villagers have taken over public forests to control grazing and timber cutting in India;[2] and in Sweden over 1.8 million acres of forest are owned by municipalities and shareholding farmers.[3] I've mentioned the timber-owning villages of Japan and the toll on them of raw log exports from the Pacific Northwest. Much closer to Coos Bay, when the logging activities of Boise-Cascade threatened their water supply, residents of tiny Williams, Oregon, mounted a campaign which has brought a temporary halt to those activities and holds the possibility of the local community's buying some of the timber giant's watershed acreage.

But communal ownership? Just a little down the road from there you come to socialism. Hardly anybody mentions such ideas anymore, when only the most gutsy politician will even call himself a liberal. "Communal ownership" must have been a slip of the keyboard.

Still, I find it interesting to ignore, for a moment, the ideological and cultural barriers to local resource ownership to focus on the practical constraints. Could Coos Bay communities have retained the earnings that have accrued to remotely based investors? This is just another way of asking whether local residents might have had the wherewithal to add value to their timber by building and running manufacturing facilities. Did the people of Coos Bay ever dream of pooling their finances and acting cooperatively to manage local resources? Probably not. But in principle, at least, investment in Coos Bay's resources and geography need not have come from private accounts.

What about the transport and marketing challenges every manufacturer must confront? The products of Coos Bay's publicly owned timber would have to compete with those of Georgia-Pacific's chain of distribution centers. They would have to swim in a sea of Weyerhaeuser Timber ads and imagery. Could local taxpayers and city managers remain aloof to the smiling goddess of high lumber prices when she beckoned them to overcut the common timber? Wouldn't they want to sell off portions of their holdings when they scraped the bottom of the public treasury and the price of wood was low?[4] But enough questions. Communal ownership of local resources seems to have at least an allergy to capitalist markets. And if we, the people of the United States can't agree on how to put the national forests to best use, what chance would a locally owned forest have?

Having said all this, I have to add that when a local community really *is* a community, rather than a collection of individuals all going their separate, private ways, anything may be possible. Local control of natural resources has become an issue in Nigeria, where people protesting environmental destruction blamed on U.S. companies' oil drilling operations have, in some cases, paid with their lives. Williams, Oregon, residents are discovering what they can do. As Marcuse put it some years ago, "The relegation of real possibilities to the no-man's land of utopia is itself an essential element of the [ruling] ideology."[5]

Did someone say, "Ruling ideology?" Whether running full-page ads, sending their economists and foresters to speak at public meetings, or creating images of forest stewardship,[6] the mostly invisible giants of the wood products industry are "masters of public relations and manipulation of the political process."[7] This according to a writer who took part in a lavish three-day, journalists' junket, at the expense of an industry think tank. As a right-wing political strategist put it in a memo to Enron executives, now come to light, "In public policy,. . .it matters less who has the best arguments and more who gets heard—and by whom."[8]

Here's a better example of just how powerful these people are. In November 2000 international representatives met at The Hague to discuss implementation of the 1997 Kyoto Protocol that addressed the problem of global warming. Despite the urgency of the problem, these talks went nowhere. Why? Because the United States, which is the largest producer of greenhouse gases, sought credit for up to half of its obligation to reduce carbon emissions by doing nothing. The U.S. argument went like this. Forests absorb carbon dioxide. The clearcuts, tree plantations, heavy use of chemicals, and genetic modification which are the stock in trade of the timber behemoths increase the volume of living matter—that is, the biomass—of trees faster than does natural forest growth. Since the United States enjoyed an abundance of these fine practices, it claimed a substantial credit for them.[9]

Now, most middle-aged Europeans have seen a lot. They are not people who are easily shocked. Nevertheless, representatives of the European Union were shocked that the United States would use such crucial talks to encourage the kind of practices that are "already threatening the earth's forests."[10] As proxy for the international forest products industry (plus car manufacturers, and oil and coal producers), the United States lost the trust of traditional allies, and no agreement could be reached.

If the power of Big Timber could influence the world's climate in potentially disastrous ways, what chance had Coos Bay? Heavily backed by Big Oil and other extractive industries, George W. Bush has now pronounced the Kyoto Protocol and its mandatory reduction of greenhouse gas emissions to be fatally flawed. But people at Coos Bay and similar depleted sites need no more evidence of corporate power than what they have experienced.

What does their experience of corporate power say about democracy in America? A citizen of legal age has the right to vote for representatives at various levels of government. But the people whose investment decisions determine whether this potential voter has the wherewithal to make the payment on the house, put food on the table, afford child care, or get the car repaired don't need his or her vote. They don't run for public office, and they can buy the loyalty of those who do. Thus, they constitute an unelected government. Is it any wonder that so many people don't bother to vote?

BACK IN 1948, when Thelonious Monk was recording "Epistrophy," the Cleveland Indians were winning the World Series, and I was celebrating my tenth birthday in our North Bend basement, William Greeley, former chief forester of the United States, wrote a letter in which he raised the all-important question for people at Coos Bay. Unless timber is cut on a sustainable basis, said Greeley, there will be "a break of many years time in the industrial life of the community." Sure, new timber growth will eventually bring new mills and jobs, but until it does, "what happens to the people, the workers, the stores and other community facilities. . . .—everything that gives American living its stability?"[11] What indeed?

But Coos Bay's problems may be worse than Greeley's letter suggests. The boom-and-bust ride on which extractive industries take local towns goes over a rocky road, but people can expect eventual relief. The hell-black night of economic bottoming *must* portend a sunny day. Or must it? The Oregon Employment Department expects "continued reductions in natural resource industries" in the Coos Bay region into the foreseeable future.[12] But maybe they just aren't looking far enough ahead.

According to a Weyco spokesman, the next "crop" of trees at their Millicoma Tree Farm will reach commercial maturity around 2010.[13] Thus, a best case scenario might see Weyco harvesting its crop that year. What then? Cutting the kind of smaller trees that may be available at Millicoma in 2010 has allowed companies to mechanize logging in amazing ways. By pushing the buttons and working the joystick of the feller-buncher, heeler-loader, stroker-delimber, or laser, a single logger of today can do what was done by a dozen not so long ago.[14] Nor can people in timber-dependent communities look to the kind of high-speed, computer-controlled mill that can produce 600,000 board feet of lumber in a week with only eighteen people on a shift to give them a lot of jobs.[15] And this is just the kind of operation a returning Weyco would be likely to run. The company's spokesman confided to me that the "glory days" of Big Timber were over. He even gave me some advice: "[y]ou'd be better off investing in CDs."[16] Thanks for the tip, but I'm invested in something else.

There is reason to doubt that the timber owners *will* come back to Coos Bay any time soon. Globalized production is opening up new sources of supplies. Corporate satellites scan Third World forests for harvestable timber stands round the clock. Stoked by Pentagon funding and Russian desperation, U.S. companies stand poised to clearcut Siberia, with its fifth of the world's forest cover.[17] We may imagine the impact on the price of wood, among other things.

Or consider this scenario for the short-term future of manufacturing jobs in the Pacific Northwest. Japan thinks that the U.S. ban on the export of unprocessed logs from public lands represents a violation of World Trade Organization rules of free trade. Should the Japanese succeed in getting the WTO to tighten these rules so as to eliminate this "trade-distorting" U.S. ban, accelerated raw log exports from the entire region could sink other mill towns to the economic level of Coos Bay.

All in all, it appears that Coos Bay and similar sites are not so much on the downside of a cycle of boom and bust as they are "at the end of an era of high-paying jobs which require little education and allow their workers to live in a low-cost community."[18] Local builder Richard Kuznitsky is struck by the waste. The area had a trained, organized workforce and a fine industrial infrastructure. The shutdown of Coos Bay's industry was "like me leaving my tools out all winter to rust," he says.

The subsurface festering of sadness and rage extends well beyond the forested regions of the Pacific Northwest, of course, as all across the industrial heartland of America, the "Fordist model" of assembly-line production by unionized labor in big company plants has been replaced by downsizing, labor "flexibility," and exported jobs. For investors, this works perfectly, but for the workers and their communities. . .well, witness Coos Bay.

IF THIS WERE A NOVEL, I'd give it a happy ending. I'd have Coos Bay's residents come together to discuss how they could start to exercise power over the life and death of their own community. Let them form committees and determine how to reach the folks who didn't show up. I'd have to end my fiction there, of course: my citizen-characters would have to write their own story—their history—from this point. But what would it be? What can the living-breathing Coos Bay people do?

Some have argued that the only way a place like Coos Bay can hope to regain control of its economic future is through local ownership and operation of its businesses. But for local consumers, "the nurturing of locally based small businesses"[19] would probably mean higher prices. For local workers, it could mean keeping out a large employer with an alluring payroll. It certainly isn't up to me to say that Coos Bay's economic independence is worth such a cost.

In fact, the possibility of establishing or re-establishing a local identity "in some sense *outside* and protected against the global flows of capital" and its empire may already be lost,[20] for there are mighty ties that bind each city, town, and hamlet to the larger whole. But the main beneficiaries of globalized production and sales operate at great remove in terms of accountability if not geography. Issues of social justice find no place at the table of the corporate elite. Coos Bay? That's how the market system operates, they shrug. They also get to name the political system. "Democracy," our elected and unelected rulers say of it.

Clearly, without a greatly heightened political awareness and level of political activity than now exists at Coos Bay and throughout the United States the decisions that determine who shall work and what will get produced—and what will get consumed and who shall pay the hidden costs—will continue to serve the needs of giant transnational corporations and their investors. Thus will the system continue to "advantage the very few at the expense of the very many."[21] But the system doesn't have to be the way it is. The Epilogue goes deeper into this.

"Every wound has its own revelation," as Normal Mailer says.[22] What do Coos Bay's wounds reveal about its future? Not much, as far as local civic leaders are concerned. When I visited the area in late 1998, there was talk of Nucor, a North Carolina-based steel manufacturer, maybe coming in. Nucor wanted a site for a steel recycling operation that would provide 250 jobs. But lacking a natural gas line and larger electrical link, Coos Bay was losing out to competing offers. In the words of a local business leader and phrase-monger, "Nucor has become a mirror into which we gaze and find the reflection isn't of a community that is prepared for major industry to come to our town, yet."[23] Refurbishing their self-image, voters subsequently approved a $20 million bond issue to bring a natural gas line to Coos Bay. By then Nucor had gone to Florida, whence the company's polluting practices came to light. Such practices could have polluted Coos Bay. Bandon's Roberta Stewart was moved to ask if the time hadn't come "to declare a moratorium on decision-making by self-appointed groups and, instead, engage the entire community in these decisions."[24] Presumably, Ms. Stewart would prefer a more democratic, less exclusionary arrangement than the $10,000 price tag (mentioned above in Chapter 8) on participation in decisions intended to "maintain and improve the region's livability."[25]

One can understand efforts to lure large, and even medium-sized, employers to Coos Bay. But such efforts indicate selective amnesia. If local residents are going to gaze into a mirror, it should be the mirror of Coos Bay's history, where they will see the twin specters of corporate plundering and dependent development. As Subcomandante

Marcos has said, "knowing oneself with history impedes one from being tossed around by this absurd machine that is the system."[26] Local leaders seek an economic solution to a *political* problem—namely, economic dependence and external control.

People have traditionally pointed to the area's physical isolation to explain Coos Bay's economic problems. The place has always been a rail link, highway or superhighway away from lasting prosperity. Recent editorials have looked to information technology to give the area a taste of urban economic growth and a foothold in the new economy. An example offered is a Coos Bay programmer with clients all over the world. Now, such a person may exist, and by now she or he may be getting rich. But can such a possibility trigger economic revitalization? What has really ridden the global highway to Coos Bay is the tech support operation I described above. (Did the *New York Times* give front-page treatment to these jobs to illustrate that the economic system corrects itself? We can only guess.)

In any case, the area was not too isolated for Weyco, Georgia-Pacific, C.A. Smith, et al. They not only found their way there but also managed to dstribute the products of Coos Bay's industry to markets and company branches all over the world. Even Asa Simpson, who had to overcome his fear of the indigenous residents, was able to find his way to Coos Bay.[27] But corporate investments linked the area's economy only to corporate needs. Remote investors got the cream. Coos Bay got a sporadic buzz of decent jobs. The Coos Bay I remember basked in the postwar glow of unprecedented demand for wood products.

ALTHOUGH IT WAS LATE DECEMBER when I last visited Coos Bay, the weather was unseasonably mild, and I took a walk around North Bend. The glittering bay reminded me of the area's efforts to attract tourists. Forest recreation creates many times the number of jobs that logging does, reportedly.[28] But that was recreation in national forests. Forests in the Coos Bay area consist mostly of enormous tree farms. For spectacular ocean scenery, tourists head for Curry County, to the south, or to coastal areas to the north. California's redwood parks draw them across the state line. Compared to what such nearby regions have to offer, Coos Bay does not hold any tourist trumps.

Disfiguring the foreground of a spot from which I wanted to take a photo of the bay was a small pile of trash. My body had once occupied that spot, for this was the very corner where, coming down the hill from school on a bike that lost its brakes, *c.* 1950, a friend and I had run into the curb. It certainly stopped the bike but it sent us flying into a hedge (no longer there), where we lay stunned but glad to be alive. I took the picture anyway.

The sun was about the *only* thing showing on the bay. Having recently noted the "Shipping News" in the local papers of forty and more years ago, I knew my memory of massive ships in port was accurate: there were often six or seven at a time. A woman at the office of the county Health Department where I vainly sought statistics said that now Coos Bay was "lucky if they get one or two ships a month." She knew because her partner tows them in.

My mind suffused with memories, I gravitated to the north end of town, strolling as far as old McCullough Bridge, where I was jolted out of my reverie by the sight of soggy bedding under it. Returning via Simpson Park, I found that Boy Scouts had improved an old familiar trail with some grades and steps. We had carried out a grim experiment combining salt and slugs in this vicinity. Here was also where I made the mistake of taunting a neighborhood girl with a broom in her hand and then turning my back. I thought of local changes that were positive, or at least benign, such as the soccer field where our softball diamond used to be, the Health Department's bilingual forms, Coos Bay's African-American sheriff ... Such changes reinforced my Rip Van Winkle sense of things.

I poked around the edge of the woods where we had spent our summer days. All was different now. People had even dumped their trash at some of the trailheads. I took a street that ended at an unexpected opening on Pony Slough. It was here that I had a customer on my early morning paper route who kept a ferocious dog. As I crept by a foot or two away, the beast would wake up with a roar and throw himself against his cage. Although I was safe, it always scared the hell out of me. The owner got his paper free, because I never even tried to collect.

Nearby I had another customer, an elderly Finn with long earlobes. When I came to collect, he would draw me into his overheated little house and make me take a chair beside him in his rocker. There I would murmur interest in his halting grievances and think that I was drowning in his medicine-laden air. He was a lonely man, no doubt, but I just wanted out of there.

Also close to here we had a rope swing on a tree that took us soaring out over the greenish muck of a swamp. It was a swamp to us, anyway, though what it really must have been was a fingernail of the slough. Now the shanties on my Portland *Journal* route and the swamp, as well, were gone, long gone, cleared out and filled in sometime in decades past, together with all trace of my father's lumberyard. A school bus yard now occupies the site.

It occurred to me that if I had stayed in North Bend this book would never have been written. Why? Because this book was inspired by a kind of shock that the long-time Coos Bay resident has probably experienced as something else, perhaps a gradual and cumulative assault on his or her sense of well-being. Considering the deterioration of local industry and the foreclosure of economic choice, Coos Bay residents have not been spared much else. As for me, I went away and then returned one day to stumble onto the scene of a crime—a crime against community.

On my last night in Coos Bay, I sit in a restaurant on the one-way street which is an increment of Highway 101. Slithering across the walls come lights of passing cars. Bright lights and Taco Time. Thursday (declares black lettering across the way): 3 Crisps/Tacos/199. Prudential wishes everyone "a great 2001 full of promise and fun," while up the street a bit the gas is 1.57/1.67/1.77. In here cigarette smoke and the sounds of a James Brown classic fill the air: "I feel nice/ like sugar and spice." But Coos Bay doesn't look as if it's feeling nice. Not anymore.

ENDNOTES

1. But local bosses and multinational corporations have gained much control over them. See John Ross [not to be confused with John R. Ross, cited above and below], "Defending the Forest and Other Crimes," *Sierra* July/August 2000: 66-71, 88.

2. See Mark Poffenberger, ed., *Village Voices, Forest Choices: Joint Forest Management in India* (New York: Oxford University Press, 2000).

3. See Katarina Eckerberg, *Environmental Protection in Swedish Forestry* (Brookfield, Vt.: Gower Publishing, 1990); Lars Carlsson, "The Swedish Forest Commons: Challenges for Sustainable Forestry?" *Sustainability—The Challenge: People, Power, and the Environment,* eds. L. Anders Sandberg and Sverker Sorlin (Buffalo, N.Y.: Black Rose, 1998) 80-89.

4. Cf. Girvan 6-7.

5. Marcuse 150.

6. Visit, e.g., <http://www.weyerhaeuser.com>.

7. Michael Harris, "News from the timber country: On tour with the American Forest Institute," *The Progressive* 44.5 (May 1980) 49.

8. Quoted by Joe Stephens, "$380,000 pitch to Enron: Bush campaign aide devised lobby plan," *San Francisco Chronicle*, February 17, 2002. (Article first appeared in the Washington Post.)

9. More recent studies cast doubt on the notion that "planting forests can be a cheap way to absorb emissions of carbon dioxide." See Andrew C. Revkin, "Forests look less promising as global warming remedy," *San Francisco Chronicle*, May 24, 2001: A8. (Reprint of article in New York Times.)

10. Jim Jontz and Aaron Rappaport, "Timber Industry Announces Plans at The Hague," email transmittal, November 21, 2000; cf. Harry Dunphy, "Warning of World Ecological Decline—Loss of political will called part of problem," *San Francisco Chronicle* 14 January 2001: A8. Also January 20, 2001: A13.

11. Quoted in Robbins, "Timber Town," 153.

12. State of Oregon, Employment Department, *Regional Economic Profile: Region 7* (Salem: OED, 11/99) 22.

13. Barnum.

14. See Don Thompson, "High-tech logging still rugged work," *San Francisco Examiner*, October 15, 2000: D-10. The content of the article belies its heading. Cf. Kent P. Connaughton, "Oregon's Local Timber Economies," in *Assessment* 199.

15. Cf. Dietrich 131.

16. Barnum

17. Parenti 100; Marchak 123.

18. Richard Gale, quoted. in Dietrich 284.

19. Edward Schwartz, "Economic Development as if Neighborhoods Mattered," *Community and Capital in Conflict: Plant Closings and Job Loss*, eds. John C. Raines, Lénora E. Berson, and David M. Gracie (Philadelphia: Temple University Press, 1982) 272.

20. Hardt and Negri 45; cf. 206 and passim.

21. Dowd 320; cf. Carl Boggs, *The End of Politics: Corporate Power and the Decline of the Public Sphere* (New York: Guilford, 2000).

22. In Norman Mailer, *The Fight* (New York: Vintage, 1997) 214, ©1975 by Norman Mailer, by permission of The Wylie Agency.

23. Portland *Oregonian*, January 15, 1990.

24. Letter, *The World*, December 30, 2000.

25. From South Coast Development Council's mission statement. See <http://www.coosbay.org/departments/econdev/scoastbusdev.html>.

26. In "Letter to Leonard Peltier," *Monthly Review* 51.8 (January 2000) 60.

27. Bancroft, *Portrait and Biographical Record of Western Oregon* (Chicago: Chapman Publishing Company, 1904) 232; Simpson, Dictation to Sessions, January 29, 1890 (Berkeley: Bancroft Library) 9.

28. See, e.g., Chad Hanson, *Ending Logging on the National Forests: The Facts* (Pasadena: John Muir Project, 1999) 6. Cf. "Uncut Forests Worth More, Lawsuit Claims," *San Francisco Chronicle*, December 18, 1998.

Who Lives There Now

WHO LIVES AT COOS BAY NOW? I think we all live there, or in the economic neighborhood. I mean, how many of us really know we won't have to spend our nights trying to sleep in a car before our days are through? Who can take anything of what we have for granted when even Social Security runs the risk of being pillaged by Wall Street? But the fact that you're reading this means you're probably *not* one of the 800,000 or so people who are homeless on any given night in America.[1] Homeless, you probably couldn't afford to buy this book, and if you went to a public library, it would probably be for shelter, not to read. But maybe I presume to know too much about other people's reading habits. The determined reader will always find a way.

Let's just hope that you have the security of a steady income. Maybe you have a good job, something offering decent pay and brighter prospects than those of workers in the seven or so assembly plants that Ford Motor Co. has announced it soon expects to close. What with U.S. employers laying off over one and a half million workers since January 2001, there have been many such announcements of late. But maybe you're self-employed. There's some security in that. The American Dream must have a waking counterpart. Of course it must, but successful self-employment requires a steady flow of clients or customers. While the spring is green, well and good, but when the pool of customers and clients who constitute your market share dries up in a recession, well, best of luck.

Perhaps you've got a cushy civil service job—or, for that matter, a grueling one. At least you have some job security, though the civil servant is the first to go when harder times descend on weaker countries that rely on first-world financing. The civil servant, too, can be laid off.

Is anyone who is not a member of the super-rich really secure? As I write, a news item whispers that graduates of business colleges no longer risk of taking jobs with smaller, start-up firms instead of more established companies. "Now it's a status symbol just to have a job," according to the publisher of a magazine for M.B.A.'s.[2] Even senior executives are out of work. Also, out of practice as they are, many of them find it difficult to conduct their own job search.[3]

While you dry your eyes over that, I have to acknowledge that the recession of the moment follows a long-lasting boom. The question is, a boom for whom? As one of my local informants remarked, the boom never got to Coos Bay. It never got to a lot of places, and it never touched the lives of millions of people. In good times and in bad, the gulf between the rich and the rest of us has been growing for the past thirty years. Note what's represented by this gulf: not just a difference in material possessions but an accelerating difference in political power. Thus do the bellies in the boardrooms of the super-rich digest more and more of the common wealth. No wonder most of those polled in 1994 no longer believed that a person could "build a better life for oneself and one's family by working hard and playing by the rules."[4] The country was crawling out of another recession at the time.

An economic boom makes for lots more jobs, but workers get a smaller and smaller slice of the expanding income pie, whose main ingredient is increased workers' productivity.[5] Adjusting for inflation, the lowest paid workers make less than their counterparts of thirty years ago. This is "globalization's dirty little secret," as one writer says.[6] While, officially, the economy was booming during recent years, employer-paid benefits were becoming a rosy memory. I'm not going to mention the vagaries of medical coverage by HMOs when most of us have at least one friend or relative who must seek treatment at an over-stretched public clinic.

Thinking of retiring? I'm concerned that fewer and fewer workers now have company-funded pension plans. In their place, employees now enjoy the dubious advantages of managing investment of a part of their earnings through 401(k) plans. The corporate meltdown that left thousands of Enron workers holding worthless company stock for their retirement is just the tip of a very slippery block of ice, as more and more people "face the risks of economic downturns on their own."[7]

Today's retiree can't even count on the provisions of a generous union contract. For every American steel worker, there are four *former* steel workers already in retirement, plus their dependents, also entitled to benefits under old union contracts. This "ticking time bomb" for the corporations that make up Big Steel has industry representatives going to the Bush administration, cap in hand, to ask for $12 billion in taxpayers' help.[8]

If your circumstances in any way resemble those of the person who has to sleep in a car or worse, I don't have to tell you that all these changes coincide with the down-sizing and elimination of government programs that, in principle at least, used to address human needs. Ten or twenty years ago, the victim of poverty qualified for food stamps, if not public welfare, but not any more. Not after "welfare reform."[9]

For anyone who *does* feel secure, what lies ahead? Because of cheerfully made decisions by the people at the pinnacle of our fossil-fuel economy, decisions that we augment every time we step on the gas, we leave a legacy of manmade climate change that will probably prove disastrous on a global scale, even for descendants of the wealthy few. Thus do we all become conspirators in a plot to tiptoe out the door with engines running and a mounting bill for someone else to pay.

If insecurity had become "a fundamental dimension of the experience of work at the end of the twentieth century,"[10] what with terrorist attacks and personal phobias it has now become a fundamental dimension of life. We not only fear to lose our jobs, we fear to fly, to open envelopes, to lose sight of our kids for a moment. Some fear what might happen if they don't display the flag; others are afraid a mob might take us off and make us kiss it! Worst of all, we fear to fight for change.

For all our fears, the question has again become: what is to be done? That's what *most* of us must ask ourselves. As for the wealthiest one percent of the world's population whose income equals that of the poorest fifty-seven percent,[11] people in that category know full well what to do: protect their gains with legislation, lawsuits, and if need be force, while sucking more and more in from everybody else. But as the *New York Times* might say, I play the class card—unlike the super-rich who own the deck!

The hard truth is that corporate capitalism, so good at bringing us innovations to increase efficiency and stock the shelves of stores with more attractive goods than we can possibly buy, requires constant economic growth. Such growth exhausts existing resources; it pollutes the environment; and it dispossesses workers left behind by resource depletion and technological change. While thrilling some with riches, capitalism has nothing to offer to the many victims of its wild ride.

Yes, there are remedies for many of our economic insecurities. National health insurance, a guaranteed living wage, and progressive tax reform jump to mind. There are also legal preventives for what happened at Coos Bay and at way too many other Coos Bays. One is plant closures legislation, laws that make it expensive for a company casually to shift its operations to a lower-cost location, thousands of miles offshore. They might still do it, but not *casually*. The problem with such legislation as a local or even state ordinance is that capital then stages a boycott, avoiding the restrictive plant-closures area as if it had a communicable disease, running the local operation into the ground, or (make that "and") tying up the local authorities in lawsuits.[12]

If it had the political will, the local community might assume control of an abandoned plant via its powers of eminent domain. Beyond the question of where do we see this happening, what could such a city—for surely it would take the resources of at least a major city—expect? Instead of researching this question, I'm just going to make a prediction, which is that long before the managers of the new public enterprise could run into problems of marketing, capitalization, or labor,[13] that bold municipality would be buried in a blizzard of legal filings. The Bard's mad monarch had it right:

Robes and furred gowns hide all.
Plate sin with gold,
And the strong lance of justice
hurtless breaks.[14]

Don't get me wrong. I'm all in favor of people battling for eminent domain. Wherever the domain is being privately abused, go after the abusers, that's what I say. People that try to put up legislative barriers to runaway factories are my heroes. Win or lose, their struggles are worthwhile for the unforgettable flashes of human solidarity that they bring. And there are personal and political lessons for anybody with the nerve to try to make a little history, instead of history always being something done to us by unknown others, sitting at their desks in far-off offices.

Let's face it though. Whether they take the form of labor rights, environmental limits on development and extraction, or protection of home industry, existing barriers to the fast flow of investments are everywhere falling, crushed by the weight of trade and investment rules prescribed by Washington's "free trade" regime. Many of us went to Seattle in November 1999 to protest the deliberations of this rule-making economic elite. We said they couldn't get away with meeting privately, without public input or accountability, to write rules that would affect us all. And for a day or two, they couldn't. But discrediting demonstrators and finding places to hold meetings far removed from any angry crowd is hardly a problem when you have the capability of holding a meeting anywhere you choose and the media to portray dissent as flat-earth ignorance.

Presently, in the spring of 2002, it looks as if a few people are working overtime to defend some fundamental rights we none of us exercise while shopping or eating or sleeping or drowning ourselves in work or entertainment. I mean, if that's all we do. . .well, you can see the problem here. Is American freedom to be freedom to shop? Of course, this is easy enough for me to ask: I hate to shop, I no longer have to work for pay, I'm not easily entertained, and I love using my First Amendment rights. It's my favorite form of exercise.

As in the world of *Beowulf*, there's a monster in our midst, an "alien entity" with a corporate charter for a body and a flood of money for its blood.[15] It's the multinational corporation that I have in mind. Not only do companies the size of Weyerhaeuser Timber and Georgia-Pacific have the power to colonize all levels of government— Enron chappies had been running large chunks of G.W. Bush's administration, it appears—but in principle they never die. Asa Simpson knew what he was doing when he turned his firm into a corporation so that his mills would go on running after he was "taken away."[16] Unless his company's holdings got sold off, which in fact they did, or the government took away his company's corporate charter, which has seldom happened since the early years of Simpson's century, those by-now refurbished mills might still be running to this day.

So, money organized to make more money, all the rights of individuals under the Constitution,[17] and immortality too: what a moxie combination for getting one's way. An honest bumper sticker on the corporate limousine might read, "We do it unaccountably." What corporate power and immortality mean for reforms is that no reform is

156

safe. As noted above, even Social Security is under attack and could become another opportunity for the few to fleece the rest of us. Thus, what reformers of one generation win, the members of a generation or two down the road have to defend. And these days when corporate capital rests its well-clad bulk on the entire world, reformers are more and more limited to defending past gains.[18]

Again: reforms are necessary, but they are not enough when, for example, successive presidential administrations are unwilling to take the kind of actions needed to head off devastating global climate change. Protecting past gains isn't enough when the system that makes economic security depend on one's having a decent job fails to provide such a job for everyone willing and able to work. A people's security is illusory when based on massive military spending and unending war.

"The arc of history bends toward justice," declared a great political leader of some thirty years ago.[19] Those words seem sadly out of tune today. If history is going to bend toward justice, we're going to have to make it bend by putting all our weight on its many branches. As you would expect, history greets such efforts just as some of us do smiling, Bible-bearing strangers at the door. "We're not interested," it says. Which only goes to show who's fashioning history. All the more reason that the only possibility I can see for a favorable outcome against the power of effectively organized money is a vastly organized people.[20]

For mutual protection, if nothing else, we need a mass democratic movement toward a new society. The success of such a movement will require hundreds of thousands and then millions of people to overcome their cultural hand-me-down of deference to authority by engaging in coordinated, nonviolent acts of insurgency,[21] and continuing to engage in such acts until the present system of corporate governance falls and a government of we the people can be formed.

Now, the fact that history offers few examples of successful mass democratic movements might mean, as conservatives have always maintained, that people aren't cut out for genuine democracy. Such experiments usually end with people's blood forming pools in the streets. I'm thinking of Paris in 1849 and 1871, Chile in 1973, Nicaragua in the early 1980s, and some other moments that started well but ended badly for adherents of democracy. But I'm also thinking of the civil rights movement in the United States and of the American Populists with their 40,000 lecturers. The record is mixed, but the bloodshed only goes to prove that the existing order, now mainly represented by the most powerful members of the world's only remaining superpower, will go to almost any length to defend itself. Consider the alternative. Do *you* think we're on the right track? I get tired of feeling politically powerless myself. So, I'm recommending something without a lot of precedents, a path filled with nettles and barbs but also human solidarity. Call it the road to democracy. We may never get there, our grandchildren may never get there, but we (they) might. And if we don't set out, it's certain that we (or they) will *never* be the citizens of a world where people have a say in the decisions that affect them commonly. In sum, democracy is a vast, untried experiment. I think we owe it to ourselves to give it a serious try. Corporate power feeds on our passivity.

Long before reaching this point, the skeptical reader will have said, "Okay, wise guy, if you're so down on the existing system, what would yours look like?" Well, part of feeling powerless in an empire that plants its colonies not only in the streets and office suites but in our minds is that it isn't easy to imagine another world. The corporate media persuade us with their every murmur that there is no other possibility. This is how it has to be. But I think there are some other possibilities.

I happen to like the bioregional utopia Ernest Callenbach portrayed in his book *Ecotopia*. I'd be hard-pressed to think up a better world than that. But in terms of ending economic insecurity, my ideal would include, at minimum, the right of everyone "to work, to free choice of employment, to just and favourable conditions of work and to protection against unemployment." Everyone would also have "the right to a standard of living adequate for the health and well-being of himself [or herself] and his [or her] family, including food, clothing, housing and medical care and necessary social services, and the right to security in the event of unemployment, sickness, disability, widowhood, old age or other lack of livelihood in circumstances beyond [one's] control."[22]

There's nothing pie-in-the-sky about such standards as these. With existing resources and technology, such guarantees could be universally realized right here on earth, but not under a regime of artificial scarcity, not when we allow a tiny minority to possess the lion's share of total income and wealth and a tyrant's share of power. Not even the law of the jungle could sanction such a maldistribution of goods and burdens as presently exists. Those rights are ours already, by the way. The quotes above are from the United Nations Universal Declaration of Human Rights. To paraphrase Eleanor Roosevelt, their destiny is in our hands.

In any case, it isn't up to me to *imagine* a better world, it's up to all of us to try to create one. That's what democracy means.

Green Party candidate for California's Secretary of State, Larry Shoup, suggests an intermediate institution in the form of democratic planning boards, one in every community or region, where elected board members would take on the task of thinking up ways to achieve full employment, among other goals. We could reasonably expect them to recommend a much shortened work week, I believe, what with everyone who was willing to work working some of the time. We could also expect such a board to recommend democratic control over investments. Think what that might have meant for Coos Bay.

But as I said, such councils represent an intermediate step. We can't begin to think of anything like that until a significant number of us turn off our televisions and begin to talk to one another about the issues that we care most about, whether jobs or health care or education or transportation or. . .you name it. That's how it has to start, and that could lead to regular meetings, research, building linkages with national and regional groups, action plans, etc. (And that's a very big "etc.") Participation in political struggle makes for personal change, which makes participation easier. But unless we take that first big step, such progress won't take place.

So, are we going to let greed out-organize human need? Will we leave the struggle for democracy to our grandchildren or maybe *their* grandchildren? The unelected government that stands behind our political representatives and their bureau chiefs can only sit on us with our consent, in the form of apathy and resignation to what already exists. Another world *is* possible, a world in which the children of people at places like Coos Bay would have as great a chance for full and free development as the children of people anywhere. It's up to us.

ENDNOTES

1. Report of National Law Center on Homelessness and Poverty, cited on the evening news, KPFA, Berkeley, Calif., January 15, 2002.

2. Quoted in Eve Tahmincioghu, "The New M.B.A. Vogue: A Job at a Blue Chip," *New York Times*, January 13, 2002: sec. 3: 12.

3. Maggie Jackson, "Executives Can Stumble at the Job-Hunt Gate," *New York Times*, January 6, 2002: sec. 3: 10.

4. Harris poll, cited by David C. Korten, *When Corporations Rule the World* (San Francisco: Barrett-Koehler, 1995) 22.

5. Jerry Kloby, "Wealth Gap Woes," *Monthly Review* 53.8 (January 2002): 59-61; cf. <http://www.ufenet.org/research/ incomecharts.html>.

6. Kelly 212.

7. Michael Sandel, Harvard political scientist, qtd. in Louis Uchitelle, "The Rich Are Different. They Know When to Leave," *New York Times* January 20, 2002: sec. 4: 5.

8. Leslie Wayne, "Parched, Big Steel Goes to Its Washington Well," New York Times, January 20, 2002: sec. 4: 1, 7.

9. Only two out of five of the parents who got such public assistance in 1995 still do, even though only a quarter of these former recipients has found a job with adequate wages to support a family. See Daniel HoSang, "From Bad to Worse: Marriage-Only Evangelists Converge on Welfare Reauthorization, *CTWO Times: News From the Center for Third World Organizing* 4.1 (December 2001) 1. See also Betty Reid Mandell, "Welfare Reform after 9/11," *New Politics* viii.4.32 (Winter 2002): 54-65.

10. Alex Callinicos, "Social Theory Put to the Test of Politics: Pierre Bourdieu and Anthony Giddens," *New Left Review* 236 (July/August 1999) 89.

11. World Bank study, cited by David Bacon, *Labor Report*, KPFA, Berkeley, January 23, 2002.

12. That was the point of G-P executive George Richie's response to Oregon's proposed plant closure legislation in 1981: "That's the kind of attitude that can only tear the state down." Quoted in *The World*, June 2, 1981:1.

13. Consider the experience of nationalization of mining enterprises in various Latin American and the Caribbean countries, as described by Girvan.

14. William Shakespeare, *King Lear* IV, vi.

15. Korten 67.

16. Simpson 1891, 15-16. Courtesy of the Bancroft Library, University of California, Berkeley.

17. In accord with *Santa Clara County v. Southern Pacific Railroad* and other Supreme Court rulings.

18. Cf. Ralph Nader, "A win today is more and more defensive," on *American Politics*, C-SPAN, February 3, 2002.

19. Martin Luther King, Jr., quoted by Joanne Macy, M.L. King Day memorial, Allen Temple Baptist Church, Oakland, Calif., January 20, 2002.

20. Cf. William Greider, *Who Will Tell the People: The Betrayal of American Democracy* (New York: Simon & Schuster, 1992) 28.

21. Lawrence Goodwyn, *The Populist Moment: A Short History of the Agrarian Revolt in America* (New York: Oxford University Press, 1978) xvii.

22. Visit <http://www.udhr.org/UDHR/udhr.htm>.

REFERENCES

Arrighi, Giovanni. *The Long Twentieth Century: Money, Power, and the Origins of Our Times.* New York: Verso, 1994.

Bacon, David. Labor Report. KPFA-FM, Berkeley. January 23, 2002.

Bakeless, John, ed. *The Journals of Lewis and Clark: A New Selection With an Introduction by John Bakeless.* New York: Mentor, 1964.

Bancroft, Hubert H. *The Works of Hubert Howe Bancroft, Volume XXX: History of Oregon, Volume II, 1848-1888.* San Francisco: The History Co., 1888. 260 ff.

—. *Portrait and Biographical Record of Western Oregon.* Chicago: Chapman Publishing Co., 1904. 232 and passim.

Barnum, Paul. Email to the author. December 4, 1998 and December 14, 1998.

Barth, Gunther. *Instant Cities: Urbanization and the Rise of San Francisco and Denver.* New York: Oxford University Press, 1975.

Baudrillard, Jean. *Selected Writings.* 2nd edn. Trans. Jacques Mourrain. Ed. Mark Poster. Stanford: Stanford University Press, 2001.

Bay, Carl. Letter. *The* [Coos Bay] *World* 27 May 1991: 4.

Beckham, Stephen D. *The Simpsons of Shore Acres.* Coos Bay: Arago Books, 1971.

—. *Coos Bay: The Pioneer Period.* Coos Bay: Arago Books, 1973.

—. *The Indians of Western Oregon: This Land Was Their Land.* Coos Bay: Arago Books, 1977.

Bensell, Royal A. *All Quiet on the Yamhill: The Journal of Corporal Royal A. Bensell.* Ed. Gunther Barth. Eugene: University of Oregon Books, 1959.

Boggs, Carl. *The End of Politics: Corporate Power and the Decline of the Public Sphere.* New York: Guilford, 2000.

Bookchin, Murray. *Remaking Society: Pathways to a Green Future.* Boston: South End, 1990.

Braudel, Fernand. *The Perspective of the World.* Trans. Sian Reynolds. New York: Perennial Library, 1986.

Brechin, Gray. *Imperial San Francisco: Urban Power, Earthly Ruin.* Berkeley: University of California Press, 1999.

Brittain, Victoria. "Colonialism and the Predatory State in the Congo." Rev. of *King Leopold's Ghost*, by Adam Hochschild. *New Left Review* 236 (July/August 1999): 133-44.

Callenbach, Ernest. *Ecotopia: The Notebooks and Reports of William Weston.* New York: Bantam, 1990.

Callinicos, Alex. "Social Theory Put to the Test of Politics: Pierre Bourdieu and Anthony Giddens." *New Left Review* 236 (July/August 1999) 89.

Carlsson, Lars. "The Swedish Forest Commons: Challenges for Sustainable Forestry?" *Sustainability—The Challenge: People, Power, and the Environment.* Eds. L. Anders Sandberg and Sverker Sorlin. Buffalo, N.Y.: Black Rose, 1998. 80-89.

Castells, Manuel. *The Rise of the Network Society.* Cambridge, Mass.: Blackwell Publishing, 1996.

Césaire, Aimé. *Discourse on Colonialism.* Trans. Joan Pinkham. New York: Monthly Review Press, 2000.

Chandler, Alfred D., Jr. *The Visible Hand: The Managerial Revolution in American Business*. Cambridge, Mass.: Belknap Press, 1977.

Cheatham, Owen R., and Robert B. Pamplin. *The Georgia-Pacific Story*. New York: The Newcomen Society, 1966.

Chomsky, Noam. "Power in the Global Arena." *New Left Review* 230 (July/August 1998) 14.

Church, Foster. "G-P shutdown affects financial, mental health of community." Portland *Oregonian*, January 26, 1981.

— "G-P's Coos Bay pullout blamed on varied factors." Portland *Oregonian*, January 26, 1981.

Cockburn, Alexander. "Save the Forests, or Gore?" *The Progressive Populist* 5.12 (November 15, 1999) 17.

Coos Bay News. June 30, 1875; August 15, 1877; June 4,1879; December 18, 1881; March 15, 1882; May 17, 1882; April 15, 1885; August 12, 1885; June 30, 1886; May 4, 1887; February 29, 1888; April 6, 1892.

Coos Bay Times. August 28, 1948: 1; August 30, 1948: 3; passim.: 1956; April 17, 1957: 1; April 8, 1959.

Corlett, Mary Lou, ed. *Forest Industries 1988–89 North American Factbook*. San Francisco: Miller Freeman, 1988.

Cox, Thomas R. "Lumber and Ships: The Business Empire of Asa Mead Simpson." *Forest History* 14.2 (July 1970): 16-26.

— *Mills and Markets: A History of the Pacific Coast Lumber Industry to 1900*. Seattle: University of Washington Press, 1974.

—, Robert S. Maxwell, Phillip D. Thomas, and Joseph J. Malone. *This Well-Wooded Land: Americans and Their Forests from Colonial Times to the Present*. Lincoln, Neb.: University of Nebraska, 1985.

Dana, Richard Henry, Jr. *Two Years Before the Mast*. Hertfordshire, England: Wordsworth, 1996.

Dietrich, William. *The Final Forest: The Battle for the Last Great Trees of the Pacific Northwest*. New York: Penguin Books USA, 1992.

Dirlik, Arif. *After the Revolution: Waking to Global Capitalism*. Hanover, N.H.: Wesleyan University Press, 1994.

Dodge, Orvil. *Pioneer History of Coos and Curry Counties, Or*. Salem, Ore.: Capital Printing, 1898.

Douthit, Nathan. *The Coos Bay Region, 1890–1944: Life on a Coastal Frontier*. Coos Bay: River West Books, 1981.

Dowd, Doug. *Blues for America: A Critique, a Lament, and Some Memories*. New York: Monthly Review Press, 1997.

Dowdle, Barney, and Steve H. Hanke in *Forestlands: Public and Private*. Eds. Robert T. Deacon and M. Bruce Johnson. Cambridge, Mass.: Ballinger, 1985.

Dunphy, Harry. "Warning of World Ecological Decline—Loss of political will called part of problem." *San Francisco Chronicle*, January 14, 2001: A8.

Earle, Chistopher J., and M.P. Frankis, eds., "Chamaecyparis lawsoniana *(A. Murray) Parlatore 1864*." <www. Conifers.org/index.htm>.

Eckerberg, Katarina. *Environmental Protection in Swedish Forestry*. Brookfield, Vt.: Gower Publishing, 1990.

Ficken, Robert E. "Weyerhaeuser and the Pacific Northwest Timber Industry, 1899–1903." *Experiences in a Promised Land: Essays in Pacific Northwest History*. Eds. G. Thomas Edwards and Carlos A. Schwantes. Seattle: University of Washington Press, 1986.

Foster, John Bellamy. "Ecology Against Capitalism." *Monthly Review* 53.5 (October 2001): 1-15.

Frachtenberg, Leo J. *Coos Texts*. Vol. 1. New York: Columbia University Press, 1913.

Frank, André Gunder. *Lumpenbourgeoisie: Lumpendevelopment: Dependence, Class and Politics in Latin America*. Trans. Marion D. Berdecio. New York: Monthly Review Press, 1972.

Georgia-Pacific Corporation. *Annual Report to Shareholders on Operating and Financial Results*. Portland, Ore.: Georgia-Pacific, *1977*.

— G-P—*Annual Report*. Portland, Ore.: Georgia-Pacific, 1978–80.

— G-P—*Annual Report*. Atlanta, Ga.: Georgia-Pacific, 1981–83.

Girvan, Norman. *Corporate Imperialism: Conflict and Expropriation: Transnational Corporations and Economic Nationalism in the Third World*. New York: Monthly Review Press, 1976.

Goodwyn, Lawrence. *The Populist Moment: A Short History of the Agrarian Revolt in America*. New York: Oxford University Press, 1978.

Gordon, Stace. Personal interview. December 28, 2000.

Greider, William. *Who Will Tell the People: The Betrayal of American Democracy*. New York: Simon & Schuster, 1992.

Hahn, T. Marshall, Jr. *Georgia-Pacific Corporation: "The Growth Company."* New York: The Newcomen Society, 1990.

Hall, Roberta L. *The Coquille Indians: Yesterday, Today and Tomorrow*. Corvallis, Ore.: Words and Pictures, 1991.

Hamper, Ben. *Rivethead: Tales From the Assembly Line*. New York: Warner, 1986.

Hanson, Chad. *Ending Logging on the National Forests: The Facts*. Pasadena: John Muir Project, 1999.

Hardt, Michael, and Antonio Negri. *Empire*. Cambridge, Mass.: Harvard University Press, 2000.

Harris, Michael. "News from the timber country: On tour with the American Forest Institute." *The Progressive* 44.5 (May 1980): 48-52.

Harvey, David. *The Condition of Postmodernity: An Enquiry into the Origins of Cultural Change*. Cambridge, Mass.: Blackwell Publishers, 1990

Heaton, Herbert. Rev. of *Timber and Men: The Weyerhaeuser Story,* by Ralph W. Hidy, Frank E. Hill, and Allan Nevins. *Forest History* 7.3 (Fall 1963): 18-19.

Hertsgaard, Mark. *Earth Odyssey: Around the World in Search of Our Environmental Future*. New York: Broadway, 1998.

Hidy, Ralph W., Frank E. Hill, and Allan Nevins. *Timber and Men: The Weyerhaeuser Story*. New York: The MacMillan Co., 1963.

Hine, Robert V., and John M. Faragher. *The American West: A New Interpretive History*. New Haven, Conn.: Yale University Press, 2000.

Hofmann, J.V. "Port Orford Cedar and Selective Logging." *The Timberman* xxiii.4 (April 1922): 66, 68, 70.

Holmstrom, Nancy, and Richard Smith. "The Necessity of Gangster Capitalism:

Primitive Accumulation in Russia and China." *Monthly Review* 51.9 (February 2000): 1-15.

HoSang, Daniel. "From Bad to Worse: Marriage-Only Evangelists Converge on Welfare Reauthorization." *CTWO Times: News From the Center for Third World Organizing* 4.1 (December 2001): 1.

Jackson, Maggie. "Executives Can Stumble at the Job-Hunt Gate." *New York Times*, January 6, 2002, sec. 3: 10.

Jacobs, Melville. "Coos Narrative and Ethnologic Texts." *University of Washington Publications in Anthropology* 8.1 (April 1939).

— "Coos Myth Texts." *University of Washington Publications in Anthropology* 8.2 (April 1940).

Jacoby, Russell. *The End of Utopia: Politics and Culture in an Age of Apathy.* New York: Basic Books, 1999.

Jontz, Jim, and Aaron Rappaport. "Timber Industry Announces Plans at The Hague." American Lands Alliance Email Press Release: November 21, 2000.

Kelly, Christine. "Muckraking in the Low-Wage World." Rev. of *Nickel and Dimed: On (Not) Getting By in America*, by Barbara Ehrenreich. *New Politics* 32.viii.4 (Winter 2002): 208-15.

Kernaghan, Charles. Interview. *Flashpoints*. KPFA-FM, Berkeley. March 26, 2002.

Kloby, Jerry. "Wealth Gap Woes." *Monthly Review* 53.8 (January 2002): 59-61.

Korten, David C. *When Corporations Rule the World.* San Francisco: Barrett-Koehler, 1995.

Kuznitsky, Richard. Personal interview. March 19, 2002.

Ladurie, Emmanuel LeRoy. *Montaillou: The Promised Land of Error.* Trans. Barbara Bray. New York: Vintage, 1979.

Langelle, Orin. "From Native Forest to Frankenforest." *Redesigning Life? The Worldwide Challenge to Genetic Engineering.* Ed. Brian Tokar. New York: Zed Books, 2001.

Lucia, Ellis. *Head Rig, the Story of the West Coast Lumber Industry.* Portland, Ore.: Overland West, 1965.

Macy, Joanne. Martin Luther King Day Memorial. Allen Temple Baptist Church. Oakland, Calif., January 20, 2002.

Mandell, Betty Reid. "Welfare Reform After 9/11." *New Politics* viii.4.32 (Winter 2002): 54-65.

Marchak, M. Patricia. *Logging the Globe.* Montreal: McGill-Queen's University Press, 1995.

Marcos, Subcomandante. "Letter to Leonard Peltier." *Monthly Review* 51.8 (January 2000): 60.

Marcuse, Herbert. *Eros and Civilization: A Philosophical Inquiry into Freud.* Boston: Beacon Press, 1966.

Marx, Karl. *Capital: A Critique of Political Economy. Vol. 1. Trans.* Ben Fowkes. New York: Vintage, 1977.

Maser, Chris. "A Sustainable Forest." *Assessment of Oregon's Forests: A Collection of Papers* Published by the Oregon State Department of Forestry. Tech. Ed. Gary J. Lettman. Salem, Ore.: Oregon State DOF, 1988. 125-33.

McGuckin, Henry E. *Memoirs of a Wobbly.* Chicago: Chas. H. Kerr, 1987.

Myrdal, Gunnar. *Development and Underdevelopment: A Note on the Mechanism of National and International Economic Inequality*. Cairo: National Bank of Egypt, 1956.

Nader, Ralph. Interview. *American Politics*. C-SPAN. February 3, 2002.

National Law Center on Homelessness and Poverty. Report. *The Evening News*. KPFA-FM, Berkeley. January 15, 2002.

Native Forest Network. *From Native Forests to Franken-Trees*. Burlington, Vt.: NFN, 2001.

New York Times. October 25, 1970; August 21, 2000.

New York Times Magazine. July 22, 2001: 31-34.

Oregon, State of, Department of Forestry. *History of Oregon's Timber Harvests and/or Lumber Production: State Data—1849 to 1992; County Data—1925 to 1992*. Compiled by Bob Bourhill. Salem: ODF, 1994.

Oregon, State of, Employment Department. *Coos Bay/Gold Beach Labor Trends*. Salem: OED, September 1998.

— *Regional Economic Profile: Region 7*. RS PUB 115-7 (11-99) Salem: OED, 2000.

Oregonian, The [Portland]. April 18, 1961: 1; April 19, 1961: 11; August 1, 1979: C22; January 26, 1981; January 15, 1990.

Parenti, Christian. "The 'New' Criminal Justice System: State Repression from 1968 to 2001." *Monthly Review* 53.3 (July–August 2001).

Parenti, Michael. *Blackshirts & Reds: Rational Rascism and the Overthrow of Communism*. San Francisco: City Lights, 1997.

Peet, Richard, with Elaine Hartwick. *Theories of Development*. New York: The Guilford Press, 1999.

Peterson, Emil R., and Alfred Powers. *A Century of Coos and Curry*. Portland: Binfords & Mort, 1952.

Poffenberger, Mark, ed. *Village Voices, Forest Choices: Joint Forest Management in India*. New York: Oxford University Press, 2000.

Pribble, Louis. Letter. *The World*, May 22, 1991: 4.

Rabelais, François. *Gargantua and Pantagruel*. Trans. Burton Raffel. New York: W.W. Norton, 1990.

Revkin, Andrew C. "Forests look less promising as global warming remedy." *San Francisco Chronicle*, May 24, 2001: A8.

Robbins, William G. *Lumberjacks and Legislators: Political Economy of the U.S. Lumber Industry, 1890–1941*. College Station, Tex.: Texas A&M University Press, 1982.

— "Timber Town: Market Economics in Coos Bay, Oregon, 1850 to the Present." *Pacific Northwest Quarterly* 75.4 (October 1984).

— "The Social Context of Forestry: The Pacific Northwest in the Twentieth Century." *The Western Historical Quarterly* xvi (October 1985).

— *Hard Times in Paradise: Coos Bay, Oregon, 1850–1986*. Seattle: University of Washington Press, 1988.

Robinson, Joan. *Aspects of Development and Underdevelopment*. New York: Cambridge University Press, 1979.

Rodney, Walter. *How Europe Underdeveloped Africa*. Washington: Howard University Press, 1972.

Ross, Gordon. Personal interview. March 19, 2002.

Ross, John. "Defending the Forest and Other Crimes." *Sierra* (July/August 2000): 66-71; 88.

Ross, John R. *Maverick: The Story of Georgia Pacific.* No place of publication: Georgia-Pacific, 1980.

Salo, Sarah Jenkins. *Timber Concentration in the Pacific Northwest: With Special Reference to the Timber Holdings of the Southern Pacific Railroad, the Northern Pacific Railroad and the Weyerhaeuser Timber Co.* Published dissertation. Columbia University. Ann Arbor: Edwards Bros., 1945.

San Francisco Chronicle, June 22, 1999; August 8, 2000: A5; January 20, 2001: A13; August 11, 2001: A5.

Schwartz, Edward. "Economic Development as if Neighborhoods Mattered." *Community and Capital in Conflict: Plant Closings and Job Loss.* Eds. John C. Raines, Lenora E. Berson, and David M. Gracie. Philadelphia: Temple University Press, 1982.

Simpson, Asa M. Dictation to D.R. Sessions, January 29, 1890. Berkeley: Bancroft Library.

— Dictation to Sessions, July 7, 1891. Berkeley: Bancroft Library.

Stephens, Joe. "$380,000 pitch to Enron: Bush campaign aide devised lobby plan." *San Francisco Chronicle,* February 17, 2002.

Stewart, Roberta. Letter. *The World,* December 30, 2000.

Sullivan, Michael D. "Oregon's Forest Industry." In Lettman, *Assessment of Oregon's Forests,* 160-68.

Sunkel, Osvald. "Transnational Capitalism and National Disintegration in Latin America." *Social and Economic Studies* 22.1 (March 1973): 132-76.

Tabb, William K. *The Amoral Elephant: Globalization and the Struggle for Social Justice in the Twenty-First Century.* New York: Monthly Review, 2001.

Tahmincioghu, Eve. "The New M.B.A. Vogue: A Job at a Blue Chip." *New York Times,* January 13, 2002: sec. 3: 12.

Thompson, Don. "High-tech logging still rugged work." *San Francisco Examiner,* October 15, 2000: D-10.

Thompson, Laurence C. and Dale Kinkade. "Languages." *Handbook of North American Indians.* Vol. 7. Ed. William C. Sturtevant. Washington: Smithsonian Institution, 1990. 30-51.

Timberman, The: An International Lumber Journal xxiii (November 1921–October 1922).

— xlix (November 1947–October 1948).

Tokar, Brian. *Earth for Sale: Reclaiming Ecology in the Age of Corporate Greenwash.* Boston: South End, 1997.

Trumpbour, John. "Greenwash and Globalization." Rev. of *The Corporate Planet,* by Joshua Karliner. *Monthly Review* 50.10 (March 1999).

"Uncut Forests Worth More, Lawsuit Claims." San Francisco Chronicle, December 18, 1998.

United Nations Industrial Development Organization. Div. of Industrial Studies. *Wood Processing Industry in a 'Timber Deficit' Country, Japan: Structural Change, Adjustment Problems and Policies.* Working Paper on Stuctural Changes: V.83-59625: August 1983.

Vance, James E., Jr. *Geography and Urban Evolution in the San Francisco Bay Area.* Berkeley: University of California Institute for Governmental Studies, 1964.

Vandelaar, Michael and Tim White. "Trouble in Mind or, Dead Fish Never Grow

Old." In *Arsenal: Surrealist Subversion*. Ed. Franklin Rosemont. Chicago: Black Swan, 1989.

Verhovek, Sam Howe. "Paul Bunyan Settling Into His New Cubicle." *New York Times*, August 21, 2000: A1, A14.

Villers, Mark W. Letter. *The World*, February 6, 1989: 4.

Wagner, Dick. *Louie Simpson's North Bend*. North Bend: North Bend News, 1986.

Walling, A.G. *A History of Southern Oregon*. Portland, Ore.: Walling, 1884.

"Warning of World Ecological Decline—Loss of political will called part of problem." *San Francisco Chronicle*, January 14, 2001: A8.

Warren, Debra D. *Production, Prices, Employment, and Trade in Northwest Forest Industries, Second Quarter 1987*. Portland, Ore.: USDA Resource Bulletin PNW-RB-147, 1987.

— .—, First Quarter 1993. Portland, Ore.: USDA Resource Bulletin PNW-RB-198, 1993.

Watson, C. B. *Prehistoric Siskiyou Island and Marble Halls of Oregon*. Ashland, Ore.: 1909.

Wayne, Leslie. "Parched, Big Steel Goes to Its Washington Well." *New York Times*, January 20, 2002: sec. 4: 1, 7.

Wedge, Sr. Augusta, Ga.: Georgia Hardwood, c. 1943.

"Weyerhaeuser." <http://www.Weyerhaeuser.com>.

Weyerhaeuser Company Annual Report. Federal Way, Wash.: Weyerhaeuser, 1984–1992.

Weyerhaeuser, George H. *"Forests and the Future": The Weyerhaeuser Story*. New York: The Newcomen Society, 1981.

World, The [Coos Bay] April 14, 1961: 14; May 15, 1961: 5, 6B; May 17, 1961: 1; May 23, 1961: 1; May 25, 1961: 2; May 29, 1981; June 2, 1981: 1; January 4, 1989; January 5, 1989; January 17, 1989: 1; January 18, 1989; January 21, 1989; February 6, 1989: 4; February 9, 1989: 1, 3; February 11, 1989; February 28, 1989; May 3, 1991: 3; May 10, 1991: 1; May 22, 1991: 4; May 25, 1991: 4; May 27, 1991: 4.

Young, John A., and Jan M. Newton. *Capitalism and Human Obsolescence: Corporate Control Versus Individual Survival in Rural America*. Montclair, N.J.: Allanheld, Osmun, 1980.

Zobel, Donald B. *"Chamaecyparis lawsoniana* (A. Murr.) Parl.-Port Orford Cedar." <http:// willow.ncfes.umn.edu/silvics_manual/ Volume_1/chamaecyparislawsoniana.htm>.

INDEX

A

African-Americans, 99,148
Akron, Ohio, 19
Alaska, 39, 127
Allegany, Ore., 123
Alpha, 29
American Federation of Labor (AFL), 101
American Populists, 157
Amsterdam, 38
Anaconda, Mont., 19
Angels Camp, 51
Antwerp, 38
Atlanta, Ga., 122
Augusta, Ga., 111
Australia, 39, 136

B

Bandon, Ore., 46, 100, 146
Beckham, S. D., 30
Beowulf, 156
Berkeley, Calif., 50, 97
Big Mill, 33, 108
Boise-Cascade Corp., 141
Bookchin, Murray, 131
Boy Scouts, 148
Braudel, Fernand, 19, 39
Brazil, 136
Brown, James, 149
Bunker Hill, Ore., 112
Bureau of Land Management (BLM), 135
Bush, George W., 143, 156

C

Caesar, Julius, 41
Callenbach, Ernest, *Ecotopia,* 63, 158
Canada, 117, 122, 125, 126, 131, 132
C.A. Smith Lumber Co., 24, 98, 100, 101, 147
Castro, Fidel, 118
Central School, 22, 102
Central Valley, California's, 38, 39
Césaire, Aimé, 56
Charleston, Ore., 49, 50
Cheatham, Owen, 107-8, 111 ff., 115, 116
Chile, 30, 136, 157
China, 39, 111
Chinese at Coos Bay, 14, 19, 29, 99, 102
Civil rights movement, 157
Cleveland Indians, 143
Coal mining, 34-36, 37, 39, 46, 60, 61
Columbia, Calif., 51
Columbia River, 28
Columbus Day storm: *see* Hurricane Freda
Communism, 101, 102
Comstock Lode, 39
Congo, 41
Congress of Industrial Organizations (CIO), 101
Constitution, U.S., 156

117, 121, 122, 125; manufacturing at Coos Bay, 24, 25, 26,
32, 34, 104, 113-15, 123-5, 132,
147; replantings, 24-5, 134, 135;
timber holdings at Coos Bay,
24-5, 26, 113-15, 117, 125, 144;
timber holdings elsewhere, 105-
7, 125; other, 98, 105-7, 108,
119, 123, 131, 142, 156
Whiskey Run, Ore., 62
White cedar: *see* Port Orford cedar
Wilcox, David, 29
Willamette National Forest, 115
Williams, Ore., 141, 142
Wilson, Woodrow, 111

Winchester, Ore., 52
Work Projects Administration
(WPA), 47
World, The, 113, 129
World Trade Organization (WTO),
144
World War I, 40, 137
World War II, 13, 22, 23, 24, 26,
101, 107-8, 115, 116, 147

Y

Yachats Prairie, Ore., 58
Youngstown, Ohio, 19
Yreka, Calif., 28, 51

More Great HANCOCK HOUSE History Titles

Big Timber Big Men
Carol Lind
ISBN 0-88839-020-3
8.5 x 11 • hc • 153 pp.

Border Bank Bandits
Frank Anderson
ISBN 0-88839-255-9
5.5 x 8.5 • sc • 88 pp.

B.C.'s Own Railroad
Lorraine Harris
ISBN 0-88839-125-0
5.5 x 8.5 • sc • 64 pp.

Buckskins, Blades, and Biscuits
Allen Kent Johnston
ISBN 0-88839-363-6
5.5 x 8.5 • sc • 176 pp.

Buffalo People
Mildred Valley Thornton
ISBN 0-88839-479-9
5.5 x 8.5 • sc • 208 pp.

Captain McNeill and His Wife the Nishga Chief
Robin Percival Smith
ISBN 0-88839-472-1
5.5 x 8.5 • sc • 256 pp.

Crooked River Rats
Bernard McKay
ISBN 0-88839-451-9
5.5 x 8.5 • sc • 176 pp.

End of Custer
Dale Schoenberger
ISBN 0-88839-288-5
5.5 x 8.5 • sc • 336 pp.

Fraser Valley Story
Don Waite
ISBN 0-88839-203-6
5.5 x 8.5 • sc • 96 pp.

Gold Creeks & Ghost Towns (WA)
Bill Barlee
ISBN 0-88839-452-7
8.5 x 11 • sc • 224 pp.

Gold Creeks & Ghost Towns
Bill Barlee
ISBN 0-88839-988-X
8.5 x 11 • sc • 192 pp.

Gold! Gold!
Joseph Petralia
ISBN 0-88839-118-8
5.5 x 8.5 • sc • 112 pp.

Great Western Train Robberies
Don DeNevi
ISBN 0-88839-287-7
5.5 x 8.5 • sc • 202 pp.

Harbour Burning
William A. Hagelund
ISBN 0-88839-488-8
5.5 x 8.5 • sc • 199 pp.

JailBirds & Stool Pigeons
Norman Davis
ISBN 0-88839-431-4
5.5 x 8.5 • sc • 144 pp.

Mackenzie Yesterday & Beyond
Alfred Aquilina
ISBN 0-88839-083-1
5.5 x 8.5 • sc • 202 pp.

Old Wooden Buildings
Donovan Clemson
ISBN 0-919654-90-8
8.5 x 11 • sc • 93 pp.

Potlatch People
Mildred Valley Thornton
ISBN 0-88839-491-8
5.5 x 8.5 • sc • 320 pp.

Quest for Empire
Kyra Wayne
ISBN 0-88839-191-9
5.5 x 8.5 • sc • 415 pp.

Walhachin
Joan Weir
ISBN 0-88839-982-0
5.5 x 8.5 • sc • 104 pp.

Walter Moberly
Daphne Sleigh
ISBN 0-88839-510-8
5.5 x 8.5 • sc • 271 pp.

Warplanes to Alaska
Blake Smith
ISBN 0-88839-401-2
8.5 x 11 • hc • 256 pp.

Yukon Gold
James/Susan Preyde
ISBN 0-88839-362-8
5.5 x 8.5 • sc • 96 pp.

hancock house

View all HANCOCK HOUSE titles at www.hancockhouse.com